LISTENING
A Practical Approach

LISTENING
A Practical Approach

James J. Floyd
Central Missouri State University

Scott, Foresman and Company

Glenview, Illinois   London, England

An Instructor's Manual is available. It may be obtained through your local Scott, Foresman representative or by writing to the Speech Editor, College Division, Scott, Foresman and Company, 1900 E. Lake Avenue, Glenview, IL 60025.

Library of Congress Cataloguing in Publication Data
Floyd, James J., 1941-
    Listening, a practical approach.
    Includes bibliographical references.
    Includes index.
    1. Listening.   2. Communication.   I. Title.
P95.46.F55   1984   808.59   84-10564
ISBN 0-673-15789-X

Acknowledgments
Chapter 1
C. J. Brown, T. R. Brown, and W. L. Rivers, *The Media and the People.* New York: Holt, Rinehart and Winston, 1978, p. 64.
From "Listening As Information Processing" by Blaine Goss in *Communication Quarterly,* Vol. 30, No. 4, Fall 1982. Copyright © 1982 Eastern Communication Association. Reprinted by permission.
Chapter 5
From "Perspectives on Classifying Nonverbal Behavior" in *Essentials of Nonverbal Communication* by Mark L. Knapp. Copyright © 1980 by Holt, Rinehart, and Winston. Reprinted by permission of CBS College Publishing.

Cover and title page
"Shell," 1927 by Edward Weston. © 1981 Arizona Board of Regents, Center for Creative Photography. In the collection of the International Museum of Photography at George Eastman House.

1 2 3 4 5 6 — RRC — 89 88 87 86 85 84

To my parents,
Joseph E. and
Mary E. Floyd

P R E F A C E

Recently, students at a large midwestern university were given a list of communication courses and asked which ones they might like to take; the one mentioned most often was the Listening course. Listening is a skill students need and one they know they need. And yet listening, more than any other communicative skill, has long been neglected. *Listening: A Practical Approach* is intended to meet that need and remedy that neglect. It can be the primary text for a course in Listening or a supplementary text for the Basic Communication course—public speaking, interpersonal communication, introduction to communication—when listening improvement is a goal. Through this book, students will gain a thorough understanding of the listening process and practical guidance for improving their listening skills.

Listening: A Practical Approach presents a skills-oriented approach to listening improvement. The first chapter addresses the importance of listening and the nature of the listening process. The next two chapters encourage students to become aware of their undesirable listening habits and to adopt a specific approach to habit modification through the three steps of recognition, refusal, and replacement. The next five chapters treat each of the specific skill areas of listening: attention, understanding nonverbal messages, understanding verbal messages, analysis/evaluation, and feedback. The final chapter explains how to apply empathic communication skills to listening behavior.

This book has a number of key features to enhance the learning experience. Learning objectives introduce each chapter, and key terms are identified at the end of each chapter. Strategically placed throughout the book are *Listening Labs,* special boxed features which focus on improving specific listening skills. A variety of interesting application exercises are included at the end of each chapter to reinforce concepts, develop skills, and encourage students to experiment with new and useful behaviors. A detailed Instructor's Manual will help implement the use of this book in your course. It includes teaching suggestions, course syllabi, additional activities, an annotated list of suggested readings, and test items.

Listening: A Practical Approach uses a variety of research findings from a broad range of areas, including listening, psychology, nonverbal communication, verbal comprehension, argumentation, feedback, and interpersonal communication. All of the material in the text has been class-tested in the listening improvement course at Central Missouri State University. Feedback from the course in the form of written analyses and evaluations has played a significant and valuable role in the writing and revising of the text.

I appreciate the invaluable assistance of a number of people throughout the two and one half years devoted to the writing of this book. Joseph T. Hatfield, Dean of the College of Arts and Sciences at Central Missouri State University, granted me release time from teaching duties. Dan B. Curtis, Chairman of the Department of Communication at Central Missouri State, was supportive in every way. I am indebted to my good friend and colleague W. Clifton Adams for his untiring willingness to discuss the project and provide valuable insights into the nature of listening. I am also grateful to Galen L. Wenger, my former colleague and outstanding speech teacher at Elkhart High School in Indiana. He first interested me in the study of listening in 1963.

I greatly appreciate the able assistance of those who reviewed the text. I owe a particular debt to Blaine Goss at the University of Oklahoma for invaluable ideas leading to revision of the manuscript. I am also indebted to my critics for their careful readings of the manuscript and their sensitive suggestions for improvement: Judy Jones, University of California, Santa Barbara; Paul King, Texas Christian University; Linda Moore, University of Akron; Bobby Patton, University of Kansas; and Deborah Hefferin Vrhel, Sauk Valley College.

At Scott, Foresman and Company, I am grateful to Michael Anderson for his assistance with early versions of the manuscript, to Barbara Muller for her support and expertise in developing the manuscript, and to Lydia Webster for her work on the final editing and for guiding the project through production.

Above all, I hope that this book will be a valuable and practical resource for all who seek to improve the important skill of listening.

James J. Floyd

C O N T E N T S

CHAPTER   3
TOWARD EFFECTIVE
LISTENING HABITS   33

CHAPTER   4
OVERCOMING BARRIERS
TO ATTENTION   45

CHAPTER 5

UNDERSTANDING
NONVERBAL MESSAGES 59

CHAPTER 6
UNDERSTANDING
VERBAL MESSAGES   74

CHAPTER   9
RESPONDING
EMPATHICALLY   118

LISTENING LABS

LISTENING
A Practical Approach

1

LISTENING: A VITALLY IMPORTANT PROCESS

OBJECTIVES

1. *To identify and understand specific reasons why effective listening is a valuable skill.*
2. *To identify and understand the costs of ineffective listening.*
3. *To acquire a basic understanding of the nature of listening and the listening process.*

Becoming a more effective listener is an exciting and rewarding experience. It is only fair to emphasize, however, that improving listening abilities is difficult, demanding, and challenging. At the very beginning it is a good idea to consider two important questions. First, are the potential benefits worth the time and effort required? Second, are there undesirable consequences, or costs, if one chooses not to become a better listener?

In addition to considering these two questions, an important element in listening improvement is developing a basic understanding of the nature of the listening process. Acquiring a definition of listening and an understanding of the components of the listening process is a good first step to take in meeting the challenge.

THE BENEFITS OF EFFECTIVE LISTENING

The average person spends about 70 percent of each day engaged in some type of communication (Nichols and Stevens, 1957, p. 6). More specifically, Nichols and Stevens report that of all the time we spend communicating each day, 45 percent is spent listening, 30 percent speaking, 16 percent reading, and only 9 percent writing (p. 6). Nichols and Stevens base these percentages on Rankin's 1926 study, but a much later study at the University of Maryland finds that people now spend 54.93 percent of their time listening, 23.19 percent speaking, 13.27 percent reading, and 8.4 percent writing (see Wolvin and Coakley, 1982, p. 5, and Werner, 1975). (See fig. 1.1.) One half or more of all our communication each day is thus spent listening.

A large portion of our listening is work related. Listening is also important in social functions, entertainment, self-enlightenment, and interpersonal relations on various levels. Regardless of the situations in which you use it, listening is definitely the communication skill you use the most. Nothing else occupies as much of your time each day. Certainly it does not seem reasonable to ignore an activity that you use so much.

In spite of the fact that we spend a great deal of time listening, we do not necessarily do it well. Like any set of skills, listening skills must be practiced correctly and appropriately. As you will discover, listening improvement is seldom easy. It requires effort, motivation, and knowledge. As Ralph Nichols (1969) warns "listening is hard work. It is characterized by faster heart action, quicker circulation of the blood, a small rise in bodily temperature" (p. 476). If you are not motivated to work at listening, you are not likely to improve. But if you understand and appreciate both the rewards of effective listening and the costs of ineffective listening, you will hopefully feel it is worth the time and effort. At this point, then, let us consider four specific benefits of effective listening: increased knowledge, job success, improved interpersonal relations, and self-protection.

INCREASED KNOWLEDGE

The world is filled with information to be consumed through listening. In fact, information is produced and exchanged at rates

Figure 1.1   Change in amount of time spent in different types of communication

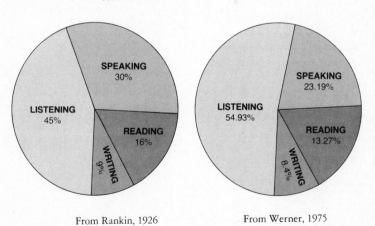

From Rankin, 1926   From Werner, 1975

faster than we ever anticipated. The rapid flow of information in the electronic age has placed us in a position in which "purely visual means of apprehending the world are no longer possible; they are just too slow to be relevant or effective" (McLuhan and Fiore, 1967, p. 63). This suggests that people will need to use listening more, not less, in the future.

Brown, Brown, and Rivers provide testimony to the fact that listening is increasing when they report that between 1970 and 1975, time spent watching television increased 40 minutes, from 139 to 179 minutes daily. Radio listening also increased, from 93 minutes to 109 minutes daily. In contrast, newspaper reading decreased 4 minutes daily, from 36 to 32 minutes. Magazine reading remained the same at 21 minutes daily (1978, p. 64). (See fig. 1.2.) It follows that since we spend increasing amounts of time in listening-related activities (television and radio), effective listening can enable us to learn more and to do a better job of analyzing and evaluating what we hear. There may actually be a reciprocal relationship between television viewing and listening improvement. Brown (1971a) discovered, for example, "that children who watch television are better listeners than those who do not" (p. 171).

Another way to understand the relationship between listening and learning is to consider how much students depend on listening.

Figure 1.2   Change in daily time spent with television, radio, newspapers, and magazines

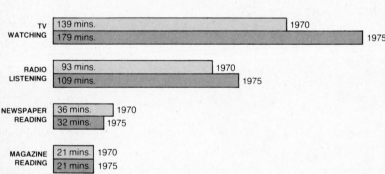

Statistics from the Television Bureau of Advertising; reported in Brown, Brown, and Rivers, 1978

As discussed earlier, the average person spends about one half of his or her communication time listening. While that fact is significant, research has shown that students in school devote even more time to listening. In an early study, Wilt (1950) found that students are expected to listen 57.5 percent of the time that they are in the classroom. Furthermore, she found that listening requires more time than "any other single activity" (p. 633). More recently, Sperry Corporation reports that students spend 60 to 70 percent of all their classroom time in listening (p. 7). Considering the amount of time spent in listening, there is no question that a student who listens effectively will learn better than one who does not. Legge (1971) supports this conclusion in his finding that students who listen effectively are more successful in their schoolwork, and that effective listeners can achieve beyond their mental capabilities as measured by intelligence tests. On the other hand, students lacking in listening skills may be "slower in developing mental abilities than those who are higher in listening ability" (p. 129).

Consider, therefore, the potential for learning that should result from improved listening. Nichols and Stevens report that in their studies at the University of Minnesota every group of students receiving instruction in listening improved by at least 25 percent, while some groups improved by as much as 40 percent (p. 15). Without instruction in listening improvement, however, it appears that the listening abilities of most people actually decline from elementary school on (Landry, 1969).

JOB SUCCESS

Increasingly, employers are looking for people who have oral communication skills. In a survey of sixty-three companies, Johnson (1971) found that "industry relies heavily upon listening as an element of communication." According to this survey, "listening affects the understanding of a problem, the retention and attention of an individual and the morale of a group" (p. 297).

In Becker and Ekdom's (1980) summary of surveys relative to the demand for communication skills, one study observed that when 282 members of the Academy of Certified Administrative Managers were requested to indicate the skills most crucial for management ability, out of twenty items, "active listening" was ranked number one and placed in the "super critical" category (pp. 14, 22).

Research by Di Salvo, Larsen, and Seiler (1976) provides additional support for the conclusion that people in business view listening as a critical factor in job success. In their survey of 170 people in business organizations, these authors asked the respondents to describe the communication skills they considered most important and that they wished they had been taught in college. In each category listening was the number one response.

Similarly, jobs in the public sector—such as governmental positions—appear to require listening ability. Speaking at the 1978 convention of the Speech Communication Association, Charlaine Hobson, of the Federal Reserve Bank of Minneapolis, indicated that the number one problem facing employees is the inability to listen effectively.

Becker and Ekdom also report that, according to employment counselors Dulin, Alderman, and Marlow, listening was at the top of a list of six communication skills that are either "quite important" or "extremely" important for successfully securing a position (p. 14). These authors surveyed numerous other studies which indicate, again and again, that oral communication skills are crucial to job success. If you recall that 50 percent of any oral communication situation involves listening, it is obvious that listening ability is a major constituent of successful employment.

IMPROVED INTERPERSONAL RELATIONS

Effective listening is important not only when you are in formal situations and job settings but also when you interact informally with friends, roommates, spouses, colleagues, and so forth. In this sense, listening skills help initiate and maintain important relationships (see Scott and Powers, 1978, pp. 227–228, 292). If you value rewarding interpersonal relationships, you need to listen effectively. Yet, as Weaver (1972) says, "it is strange that most people do not really want to listen, but to talk" (p. 82). Accordingly, if everyone talks and no one listens, interpersonal relations suffer. So, to the extent that being listened to is a human need, it makes sense to listen well.

If you stop to consider the extraordinary complexity of the world in which we live, it is not difficult to understand why humans need to be listened to. In the age of television, radio, computers, telephones, and the rapid transportation of people and information, there are indeed many speakers and countless messages. But it is difficult to find people who are simply willing and able to listen. Learning to listen can perhaps do more to help others than any other communication skill. In turn, effective listeners receive the benefits of learning from others as well as understanding themselves better. As Rogers and Roethlisberger suggest, "good communication, free communication, within or between men, is always therapeutic." And a major factor in such communication is the ability "to see the expressed idea and attitude from the other's point of view, to sense how it feels to be him, to achieve his frame of reference in regard to the thing he is talking about" (Rogers and Roethlisberger, 1952, pp. 46–47).

SELF-PROTECTION

The great British statesman Edmund Burke once said, "all that is necessary for the forces of evil to win in the world is for enough good men to do nothing." In a free society there can be only the most limited legal restrictions on the freedom to speak. To do otherwise would be to destroy one of our most fundamental rights. As Johannesen (1983) suggests, "our society applies ethical standards for communication through the more indirect avenues of group consensus, social pressure, persuasion, and formal-but-voluntary codes of ethics" (p. 86). Thus, we must thoroughly understand that not all speakers have our best interests at heart. Those who are tricky and deceptive, those who are poorly informed, those who disguise weak logic and lack of evidence through effective delivery and emotional appeals, and those who are more interested in personal gain or advantage than in the welfare of others are free to speak in our society. Protection from such speakers must come, not through attempts to put an end to "bad" speakers, but through our ability to become active, capable listeners who understand, analyze, evaluate, and respond effectively. As Larson has urged, "our most important activity as human beings in a democratic society is to become critical and knowing consumers of information." He adds that this is particularly true "of information that seeks to advise us to certain courses of action" (1973, p. 5). Understanding the listening process and striving to become a more effective listener are vitally important means of doing what Larson urges.

THE COSTS OF INEFFECTIVE LISTENING

Another way to understand the importance of listening is to consider the costs of ineffective listening. It is encouraging to note, for example, that business leaders are beginning to understand that poor listening is costly—economically and personally. Sperry Corporation, for instance, has engaged in a program designed to teach listening skills to their employees. Officials at Sperry recognize that listening is a basic skill, and that it is a neglected subject in schools. Furthermore, they realize that listening problems add up to millions of dollars in losses—losses caused by the avoidable problem of poor listening. Accordingly, "with more than 100 million workers in America, a simple ten dollar listening mistake by each of them would cost a billion dollars." As a result, "letters have to be retyped; appointments rescheduled; shipments reshipped." Sperry concludes that the failure of people to listen to one another results in the distortion of ideas "by as much as 80 percent as they travel through the chain of command." As a result, "employees feel more and more distant, and ultimately alienated, from top management" (p. 8).

In 1973, and again in 1976, the Undergraduate Studies Committee of the American Business Communication Association surveyed student opinion of the basic communication course. Students recommended less time on "letter writing and long report writing." They recommended that more time should be devoted to oral communication, including more time on listening (Huseman, Lahiff, and Hatfield, 1981, p. ii).

Ineffective listening and lack of instruction in listening are significant problems in our society. Students enjoy less success in school because of the inability to listen (Brown, 1971b). The absence of skills in listening is related to slower development in mental abilities, while effective listening is related to success in learning (Legge, 1971). And Lundsteen indicates that there is a need for broader focus on problem solving and critical thinking as a means of overcoming problems in critical listening ability (1971, p. 246).

In virtually every facet of life poor listening proves costly. Opportunities are lost. Time is wasted. Misunderstandings occur. More seriously, patients are given the wrong medication and airplane pilots misunderstand instructions from the control tower (see Steil, Barker, and Watson, 1983, pp. 40–41). In these examples and countless others failure to listen carefully and accurately proves costly.

It is difficult to find anyone who has gone through the American educational system without having numerous classes in reading and writing. It would be equally difficult to find anyone who has had a single course in listening. Somehow, we have repeatedly exposed people to reading, writing, and arithmetic, yet, we do not teach people how to listen more effectively. Until this situation is changed significantly, the majority of people will continue to listen poorly and continue to suffer in a variety of ways as a result.

LISTENING DEFINED

Defining listening is not an easy task. As Wolvin and Coakley (1982) remind us, *"the* definition of listening is still in the process of being developed."* They also remind us that research in listening is in an exploratory state, and much of it has yet to be "coordinated or collated" (p. 30). At the present time, then, it may not be possible to present a definition of listening satisfactory to everyone.

In a general sense, listening may be defined as a *receiver orientation to the communication process:* since communication involves *both* a source and a receiver, listening consists of the roles receivers play in the communication process. Some scholars, such as Weaver (1972) and Spearitt (1962), describe listening as a singular, distinct activity, but I maintain that listeners perform a variety of closely related behaviors in fulfilling the receiver function in communication.

Specifically, listening is a process that includes *hearing, attending to, understanding, evaluating, and responding to* spoken messages. This definition does not exclude attending to and understanding visual stimuli. In short, this definition assumes that listeners should be active participants in the communication process, and that listening improvement occurs as listeners learn to perform each of these behaviors more effectively.

Since developing an understanding of the listening process represents an important first step in realizing the benefits of effective listening and avoiding the costs of ineffective listening, some understanding of the basic components of listening should prove helpful.

HEARING

Hearing is essentially a matter of receiving sounds. It requires properly functioning ears. The basic parts of the ear are illustrated in figure 1.3. As Lindsay and Norman (1977) indicate, the ear is a complex instrument. It does not merely receive and record sounds. Instead, aural signals go through several changes before reaching the brain. Essentially, sound waves travel through the air and into the auditory canal. The vibrating air strikes the eardrum, and the sound enters the inner ear through bone conduction. It is then conducted through liquid in the cochlea and is sent to the brain by way of the auditory nerve.

If your hearing is normal, you should be able to receive sounds without difficulty. There are, however, several conditions which can adversely affect your hearing. These may consist of physical problems which can lessen or even destroy hearing: masking, a condition in which sounds are "drowned out" by other sounds; problems in auditory discrimination, or distinguishing between sounds; and auditory fatigue, a condition which can result from exposure to a monotonous, repetitive sound (see Lundsteen, 1971, pp. 23–26, 35).

Significantly, the absence of such hearing problems does not mean that a person is listening. You may physically hear sounds but pay no attention to them whatever. Thus, listening is a voluntary behavior, while hearing is much less so. This has led some authorities to question whether hearing is actually part of the listening process or simply "a necessary condition" for it (Wolvin and Coakley, 1982, p. 40). Essentially, hearing is only the beginning of the listening process. It is a mistake to equate it with listening.

A COGNITIVE MODEL OF LISTENING

The next step in understanding the listening process is to consider the cognitive processes involved in perceiving and comprehending messages. This can be accomplished by examining Goss' (1982) Model of Listening. As apparent in figure 1.4, Goss indicates that listening involves three levels of processing: signal processing

Figure 1.3   Parts of the ear

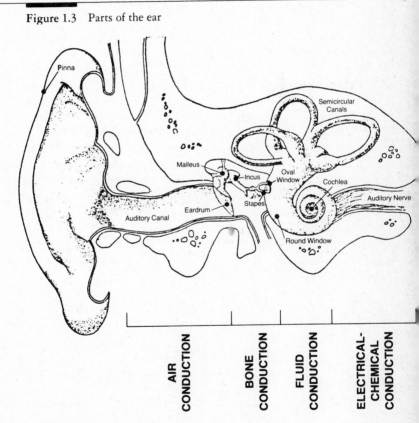

From *Human Information Processing,* Second Edition, by Peter H. Lindsay and Donald A. Norman. Copyright © 1977 by Academic Press, Inc. Reprinted by permission.

(SP), literal processing (LP), and reflective processing (RP). Added to the bottom of Goss' model in figure 1.5 are the four skill areas of listening as they correspond to the three types of processing. This model should help you to understand that *perception, comprehension, evaluation, and response* are important aspects of listening.

SIGNAL PROCESSING (SP)

As the Goss model indicates, the first step in listening is signal processing. In this step the listener "begins the language process task" by engaging his or her "language competence to understand the phonetic, syntactic, and semantic characteristics of the message" (Goss, 1982, p. 305). The essential requirement for signal processing is *knowledge of the language being spoken*. Without such knowledge, the various sounds of speech will seem to run together into a meaningless flow of sounds which you cannot process meaningfully. If this happened, you would not be able to proceed to literal or reflective processing of the message. You would most likely give up, concluding that "it didn't make sense; it was jibberish."

Fortunately, signal processing poses relatively few problems in your daily communication. Knowing the language spoken and being exposed to reasonably clear speech, you probably encounter few problems with this aspect of listening. On the other hand, were you to take a trip to London and meet people who speak English with a

Figure 1.4 Goss model of listening

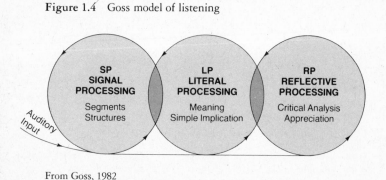

From Goss, 1982

cockney accent or visit a European country in which you are unfamiliar with the language spoken, you would become very much aware of signal processing problems.

LITERAL PROCESSING (LP)

The second type of processing is literal processing. According to Goss (1982), "It refers to the initial assessment of meaning to the message parts by the listener" (pp. 305–306). Literal processing is a matter of understanding the *denotative meanings that the words represent.* In everyday communication you may encounter relatively few problems with literal processing. If someone says, "Please move that empty box out of the way," you could probably do so without having to spend much time figuring out the speaker's meaning.

At times, however, a speaker may use words which are not familiar to you, or which are ambiguous and confusing. Suppose someone were to say, "Meet me at the union at 3:00 P.M." If you think "union" refers to the student center on a college campus, while the speaker is thinking of a labor union building, you will be experiencing difficulty in literal processing.

Figure 1.5   Goss model of listening with steps of listening process

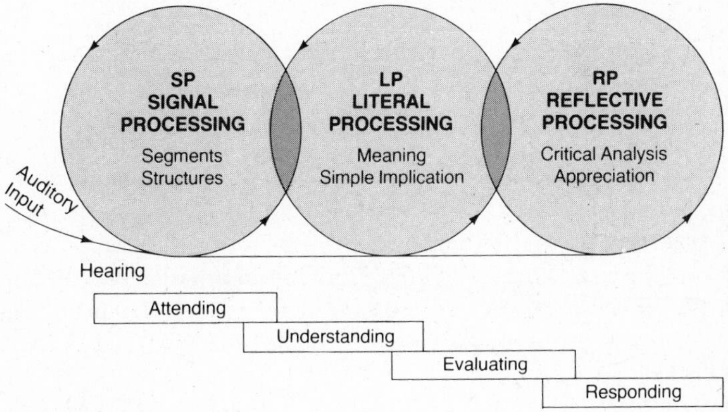

Adapted from Goss, 1982

REFLECTIVE PROCESSING (RP)

Reflective processing occurs "once the listeners have a basic understanding of the message." It is "deeper than literal processing in that listeners think about the message, make more inferences, evaluate and judge the speaker and the message, etc." (Goss, 1982, p. 306). It is reflective processing that Lundsteen (1971) associates with appreciative and critical listening. Thus, in processing messages reflectively, the listener attempts to understand the message thoroughly, drawing conclusions about the message and making evaluations of the speaker and his or her message.

In summary, the three levels of information processing in Goss' model include *signal, literal, and reflective processing.* As Goss indicates, the listener "can engage in all three parts simultaneously, especially when focusing on different segments of a continuous message." It is also "possible that the listener would not process a message beyond the LP level" (p. 306).

It is important to note, also, that Goss' model accounts for each of the parts of the listening process—Attending, Understanding, Evaluating, and Responding. This model should help you to understand that while the steps of the listening process may be considered separately, they actually overlap and interrelate. In later chapters we will consider the skill areas of listening, focusing on how you can more effectively perform these skills by overcoming undesirable habits that pose barriers to listening improvement.

A CHALLENGE

We have considered the importance of listening in everyday life and the impact of the information explosion in our time. In light of these two facts, I strongly urge you to accept the challenge of improving your listening abilities. With the information provided in this book and your serious attempt to strive for improvement, you can expect to profit greatly from the benefits of improved listening skills.

REFERENCES

Becker, S. L. and L. R. V. Ekdom. "That Forgotten Basic Skill: Oral Communication." *Association for Communication Administration Bulletin* 33 (1980), 12–25.

Brown, C. T. "Listening Ability and Radio and Television Habits." In *Listening: Readings,* S. Duker, ed. Metuchen, N.J.: Scarecrow Press, 1971a, 170–173.

Brown, C. T. "Relationships Among Listening, Reading, Intelligence, and Scholastic Achievement." In *Listening: Readings,* S. Duker, ed. Metuchen, N.J.: Scarecrow Press, 1971b, 94–99.

Brown, C. J., T. R. Brown, and W. L. Rivers. *The Media and the People.* New York: Holt, Rinehart and Winston, 1978.

Di Salvo, V., D. C. Larsen, and W. J. Seiler. "Communication Skills Needed by Persons in Business Organizations." *Communication Education* 25 (1976), 269–275.

Goss, B. "Listening as Information Processing." *Communication Quarterly* 30 (1982), 304–307.

Hobson, C. Federal Reserve Bank of Minneapolis. Speech presented at Speech Communication Association Convention, Minneapolis, November, 1978.

Huseman, R. C., J. M. Lahiff, and J. D. Hatfield. *Business Communication.* Hinsdale, Ill.: Dryden Press, 1981.

Johannesen, R. L. *Ethics in Human Communication.* 2nd ed. Prospect Heights, Ill.: Waveland Press, 1983.

Johnson, J. D. "A Survey of Listening Programs of a Hundred Major Industries." In *Listening: Readings,* S. Duker, ed. Metuchen, N.J.: Scarecrow Press, 1971, 288–301.

Landry, D. L. "The Neglect of Listening." *Elementary English* 46 (1969), 599–605.

Larson, C. U. *Persuasion: Reception and Responsibility.* Belmont, Calif.: Wadsworth, 1973.

Legge, W. B. "Listening, Intelligence, and School Achievement." In *Listening: Readings,* S. Duker, ed. Metuchen, N.J.: Scarecrow Press, 1971, 121–133.

Lindsay, P. and D. Norman. *Human Information Processing.* 2nd ed. New York: Academic Press, 1977.

Lundsteen, S. *Listening: Its Impact on Reading and Other Language Arts Skills.* New York: National Council of Teachers of English, 1971.

McLuhan, M. and Q. Fiore. *The Medium Is the Massage.* New York: Bantam Books, 1967.

Nichols, R. G. "Listening Is a 10-Part Skill." In *Readings in Interpersonal and Organizational Communication,* R. C. Huseman et al., eds. Boston: Holbrook Press, 1969, 472–479.

Nichols, R. G. and L. Stevens. *Are You Listening?* New York: McGraw-Hill, 1957.

Rankin, P. T. "The Measurement of the Ability to Understand Spoken Language" (unpublished Ph.D. dissertation, University of Michigan, 1926). *Dissertation Abstracts* 12, No. 6 (1952), 847–48.

Rogers, C. R. and F. J. Roethlisberger. "Barriers and Gateways to Communication." *Harvard Business Review* 30 (1952), 46–52.

Scott, M. D. and W. G. Powers. *Interpersonal Communication: A Question of Needs.* Boston: Houghton-Mifflin, 1978.

Spearitt, D. *Listening Comprehension: A Factorial Analysis.* Melbourne, Australia: Australian Council for Educational Research, 76, 1962.

Sperry Corporation. "Your Personal Listening Profile."

Steil, L. K., L. Barker, and K. W. Watson. *Effective Listening: Key to Your Personal Success.* Reading, Mass.: Addison-Wesley, 1983.

Weaver, C. *Human Listening: Processes and Behavior.* Indianapolis: Bobbs-Merrill, 1972.

Werner, E. K. "A Study of Communication Time" (M.A. thesis, University of Maryland—College Park, 1975), p. 26.

Wilt, M. E. "A Study of Teacher Awareness of Listening as a Factor in Elementary Education." *Journal of Educational Research* 43 (1950), 626–636.

Wolvin, A. D. and C. G. Coakley. *Listening.* Dubuque, Iowa: Wm. C. Brown, 1982.

KEY TERMS

Listening

Hearing

Understanding

Analyzing/evaluating

Responding

Signal processing

Literal processing

Reflective processing

EXERCISES

1. Ask three of your friends who have never taken a course in listening to tell you what they think listening is and how important it is in comparison to reading and writing. Compare and contrast their responses in relation to the definitions of listening presented in this chapter.

2. Interview a person who holds a responsible position in a business or a profession. Seek this person's views concerning the importance of listening in employment interviews, job success, and supervision of employees.

3. Begin a daily notebook or journal in which you comment on listening as you observe it day by day. Note your own listening problems and those of others. Record your successes and progress in listening.

4. Assume that you hear a speaker say, "If you do not jog regularly, you are four times more likely to have a heart attack than if you do jog regularly." Explain the literal meaning of the statement. Also explain possible meanings which might result from reflective processing.

5. Discuss ways in which this chapter suggests that listeners and speakers share equally in the responsibility to achieve effective communication.

2

INEFFECTIVE
LISTENING
HABITS

OBJECTIVES

1. *To understand the relationships between listening and habits.*
2. *To understand and to identify habits which interfere with effective listening.*
3. *To begin identifying your undesirable listening habits.*

A person may drive an automobile for years without becoming a good driver. Likewise, a teacher may teach classes day after day, year after year, without ever improving significantly in his or her ability to teach effectively. People who do not learn to perform any skill well, may very likely fall into the trap of becoming habituated to a poor performance level. It may simply never occur to them that there is a problem.

Listening is a good example of such a skill. We have been doing it all our lives, probably giving little thought to our ability to listen effectively. And, more likely than not, we have been devoting a lifetime to establishing undesirable listening habits. Studies in listening competency indicate that this is precisely what happens. Nichols and Stevens have done extensive research in listening, and they have discovered that, on the average, we listen at only a 25 percent efficiency (1957, p. ix). Moreover, their research "has been substantiated by reports of research at Florida State University, Michigan State University, and elsewhere" (pp. 5–6).

It should be emphasized that the research reported by Nichols and Stevens relates to the inability of people to remember what they have heard. Nonetheless, such research suggests the probability of a number of serious listening problems. As we shall discuss in chapter 4, inattention frequently makes it difficult to retain information. Additionally, *the failure to understand what one hears, the functioning of undesirable habits, lack of motivation,* and *careless, hasty evaluation* are listening problems which can adversely affect one's ability to remember.

THE IMPORTANCE OF HABITS

Mursell defines habits, first, as "instrumentalities," or "techniques for dealing with some life problem, for achieving or trying to achieve some life purpose." Second, he defines habits as "a standardized method of trying to achieve some definable satisfaction" (1953, p. 27). His definitions suggest that habits involve a repeated way of dealing with given situations. They become so well established, or "standardized," that we perform them without consciously thinking about it. Rachlin expresses this when he says that "habituation is nothing more than getting used to something." A habit is "by its very nature" a behavior which "we do not notice" (1976, pp. 103–104).

As Hasher and Zacks (1979) have suggested, some processes require considerable conscious effort ("effortful processes"), while others require minimal conscious effort ("automatic processes"). Listening habits, like many other habitual behaviors, are often automatic. When you put your socks and shoes on each morning, you probably start with either the right or left foot each time. Yet, as with most people, you probably could not say which foot you begin with. Similarly, most people cannot easily account for their daily listening habits, particularly those which have been established over time to the point of becoming habitual, effortless behaviors. This fact is important in understanding how we develop poor listening behaviors. It does not, however, mean that we habitually respond to each listening situation in the same way. Instead, we tend to develop habitual ways of dealing with similar types of listening situations. Catania (1973) refers to this as "habit-family hierarchy" (p. 32). Poor listening habits may develop in some situations but not in others. But we may also establish general patterns of listening which may apply most of the time.

We must keep in mind, however, that most of us need to be concerned about changing these poor habits. As previously discussed, there are numerous indications that people do not listen effectively. If you want to become a better listener, you should begin by becoming aware of the characteristics of poor listening.

HABITS RESULTING FROM ROLES

Some undesirable listening habits result from confusion over the roles speakers and listeners should perform in the communication process. Let us consider two important sources of such confusion. The first concerns the tendency to talk instead of listening.

Listeners who do this habitually spend most of their time formulating what they are going to say next and looking for an opportunity to say it. The second area of speaker-listener role confusion involves the tendency to view listening as a passive behavior. In passive listening, people tend to assume that communication is totally the speaker's responsibility.

THE TALKER

Communication is a process which requires listeners as well as speakers. While this may strike you as too obvious to deserve mention, poor listening frequently occurs, especially in interpersonal and small group settings, when everyone prefers to talk rather than to listen. To function as an effective listener, you should be willing to listen carefully enough to understand and to appreciate the speaker's ideas and feelings. This is difficult to accomplish when you are interested in what you are going to say as soon as the next opening occurs.

Effective listening requires concentrated effort on your part to understand the speaker prior to framing your response. If you are more interested in talking than listening, problems will develop. As Weaver (1972) says, "most people do not really want to listen, but to talk" (p. 82). Barker (1971) discusses the same basic problem when he says that "we think we know what the speaker is going to say and begin formulating mental or oral questions with regard to the projected message, or perhaps a great 'comeback.'" He adds that "this habit, at times can make listeners appear foolish, rude, or not very bright" (p. 63).

Unfortunately, we often love to hear the sound of our own voices and feel that nothing anyone else has to say could possibly be as accurate or as interesting as our statements. So, instead of listening carefully to the speaker we spend most of our time formulating our next statement—even when we are in situations in which it will be unlikely that we will be able to speak. If we cannot overtly respond, we opt to create a running, internalized speech or debate. This is poor listening simply because it prevents us from understanding the speaker. Quite frequently, we may appear to listen carefully to the speaker while internally missing most or significant parts of the message. This problem will be discussed further in chapter 4.

THE PASSIVE LISTENER

Recently, a group of intelligent students were asked, "What is good literature?" One student replied that good literature is any literature which educated, intelligent people will recognize as having the qualities of beauty and truth. A second student said that good literature is whatever a person enjoys reading. A third student responded by saying that good literature is that which withstands the test of time and which people generally agree is good. Clearly, these three students had different meanings for the same expression, and if they failed to consider the differences, they might have assumed that each person had similar meanings for "good literature."

Listeners often think that listening is passive, requiring only that they can sit back and take in the speaker's message. Somehow they think that meaning resides inherently in words. Such assumptions are troublesome. Ehninger, Gronbeck, and Monroe (1980) tell speakers that

> because words are merely symbols which stand for the concepts or objects they represent, your listener may attach to a symbol a meaning quite different from the one you intend. (p. 159)

A speaker has no reason to assume that listeners will assign meaning to the message that is the same as the intended meaning. Thus, it is the *speaker's* responsibility to select words which will mean the same to listeners as they do to the speaker. Indeed, this is good advice for speakers who do not want to be misunderstood.

On the other hand, as *listeners* we must realize that speakers may not always follow this advice. If we are too ready to accept the idea that words mean whatever we want them to mean, and that we are free to assign whatever meanings we wish to a speaker's words, then we are going to have listening problems. Assume, for example, that you are listening to someone who says that a report should be "perused," and you conclude that the speaker is asking you to glance through it or skim it; you may have made a serious listening error. If the speaker is thinking of the dictionary meaning of "peruse," then he or she is asking you to read the report carefully, to study it.

In chapter 6 we will examine ways to minimize such problems. For the present, however, you should realize that it is unreasonable to conclude that listeners can attach whatever meanings they wish to a speaker's words and assume that they are listening accurately and fairly. As Sperry Corporation indicates, listening is just as active as talking, although most people believe the primary responsibility for good communication rests with the speaker. "Think how much better we could communicate if both the listener and the speaker took at least 51 percent of the responsibility for successful communications!" (p. 8). Effective listening requires effort. Passive listeners cannot expect to understand much about the speaker or the message.

ATTITUDINAL HABITS

Poor listening results from numerous factors. Frequently, it is caused by problems within the listener (attitudes) or problems within the listening situation. Effective listeners should be aware of such problems and make sustained efforts to overcome them.

THE ENTERTAINMENT SYNDROME

A major characteristic of poor listening is the demand that all speeches and speakers be interesting or entertaining before they deserve one's time and attention. For example, Stroh (1971) indicates "interest" and "novelty" as two of the factors of focus and attention (p. 1). It is, therefore, extremely easy to develop the habit of rejecting messages that lack novelty or interest and speakers who do not satisfy our need for entertainment.

One might reasonably argue that an effective speaker has a responsibility to adjust to the audience and to make the subject interesting enough that listeners will be motivated to pay attention. As tempting as it may be to use such reasoning as a justification for not listening, it does not satisfactorily address the problem of ineffective listening. Let us consider two examples of situations in which you might function as a listener. In the first instance the speaker is highly entertaining, telling numerous jokes and entertaining stories. This speaker's delivery is animated, forceful, and varied. While the topic is not developed well and provides little useful information, you leave the presentation feeling that it was interesting and fun. You might not have learned much, or you might have received watered down, overly simplified information, yet you comment on what a good speaker this person was.

In the second instance the speaker is not at all entertaining. Delivery is monotonous and colorless. This speaker's voice is too soft, forcing you to strain in order to hear. Yet this speaker presents solid, useful information. You may not have listened to much of it, but the message was substantive and well-supported. You excuse your poor listening by finding fault with the speaker, commenting on the dull, uninteresting delivery.

One might object to these two examples by pointing out that these speakers are extreme examples. There are, after all, speakers who deliver excellent content in an interesting, entertaining manner. Certainly there are such speakers. They represent an ideal in that they keep us entertained at the same time that they present worthwhile messages. Unfortunately, however, such speakers are probably the exception rather than the rule, and if you demand such excellence

---

Listening Lab

Inventory of Poor Listening Habits

* Being preoccupied with talking not listening
* Predicting what the speaker will say
* Formulating response prematurely
* Using ambiguous words
* Assigning the wrong meaning to words
* Avoiding uninteresting material
* Distorting messages due to bias
* Oversimplifying answers or explanations
* Yielding to external distractions
* Yielding to internal distractions
* Avoiding difficult or demanding material
* Rationalizing poor listening

before you are willing to listen, you are exemplifying the entertainment syndrome.

The basic issue is this: when it is to your advantage to listen well, can you afford to justify poor listening because your entertainment needs are not met? Perhaps we need to ask whether we are actually serving our own best interests when we daydream, talk to others, sleep, and so forth, simply because the speaker is "dull" or the topic is "boring." It might pay to listen to dull speakers. If your boss is explaining information about new procedures that will directly affect the way you are expected to do your job, failure to listen carefully because he or she is a dull, monotonous speaker will probably prove costly to you. Whether the speaker is interesting or not, it is to your advantage to listen carefully.

LISTENING THROUGH BIASES

Everyone has biases, which simply means that we all have preferences, likes, and dislikes. If, for example, you think that cheating is wrong you could say that you are biased against cheating or biased in favor of honesty. Inherently, there is nothing wrong with bias. It certainly is unreasonable to think that anyone can ever become totally objective, or that anyone can cast aside personal experiences and feelings. Our attitudes, beliefs, and values are part of us and are going to affect our thinking and responses in practically every listening situation. As Makay and Brown explain it, the listener, or receiver, of a message "interprets the symbols and messages," measuring "these stimuli against his knowledge, attitudes, and values to experience comprehension and some sort of acceptability or rejection" (1972, pp. 268–269).

The difficulty arises when biases function to distort the message received from the speaker. In order to illustrate this potential problem, let us assume that one of us is listening to a friend who is talking about abortion. Let us assume, further, that the listener's religious training has taught him or her that abortion is a mortal sin, that it is exactly the same thing as murder, and that it is never justified. The person speaking is also opposed to abortion but not as strongly as the listener. At one point early in the discussion the speaker says that we have to have some understanding for people who sincerely believe that abortion is a matter of personal choice. At this point the listener may reject the speaker, deciding that he or she is in favor of abortion on demand and is, consequently, an immoral person.

This response may negatively affect the listener throughout the remainder of the conversation. Our listener may begin to distort the rest of the speaker's remarks in a variety of ways:

1. By simply not processing some of the content

2. By insisting that the speaker made statements or took stands which he or she did not take

3. By deleting message elements, or by adding or inserting elements into the message that were not there

4. By deciding that any anti-abortion statements were not sincere or were stated simply to throw the listener off guard

Makay and Brown (1972) label these types of biased responses as "filtering," "assimilation-contrast," "deletion-addition," and "rationalization" (p. 127).

These poor listening processes may operate positively as well as negatively. If, for example, a group of labor union members strongly support a leader, they may continue to support the leader even when hearing verified, carefully documented evidence establishing that he or she has connections with organized crime, has mishandled union funds, and has lied in sworn testimony. Sympathy for this person may lead listeners to respond to such statements by asserting that "big business" is fabricating charges against union leadership in order to "break the union." They may decide that governmental agencies are acting against their leader out of political motives. They may also search for examples of generosity and unselfishness on the part of the leader and conclude that such evidence disproves the case against their leader.

Even though we all have biases, and even though they are sometimes desirable, when they interfere with our ability to attend to, understand, and evaluate a message accurately and fairly, they become a factor in poor listening. Although we cannot rid ourselves of all our biases, we can learn to minimize the tendency to let them stand in the way of effective listening.

UNCRITICAL LISTENING

This characteristic of poor listening may seem contradictory to much of the discussion so far in this chapter. For, if poor listeners tend to judge without understanding and reject speakers who are not entertaining, how can we now describe them as not being critical enough? The point of this section relates to the practice of some speakers who give the impression of fulfilling all listener needs and expectations. Such speakers appear to make difficult, complex issues simple and easy to understand. They reinforce the desire of listeners to have a good time. Waldo Braden, former Chairman of the Department of Speech at Louisiana State University, once referred to such speakers as dispensers of "snake oil." Says Braden (1969), these speakers attempt to fulfill a desire "for short cuts and gimmicks in the art of communication" (p. 181).

When you recall, then, that ineffective listeners like to be entertained, and desire to have their biases and prejudices reinforced rather than challenged, you should begin to see how uncritical listening becomes a problem. Let us assume, for example, that a person hates doing various household chores. We can imagine how uncritically receptive this person might be to commercial messages which claim to eliminate the need for performing such chores or which promise to make them easy and effortless. Or, consider how frequently people are receptive to conspiracy theories that grossly oversimplify difficult, multifaceted problems. When, for instance, Americans must face up to years of wasteful exploitation of a limited natural resource like oil, many of them love to hear speakers blame the entire problem on the major oil companies.

If listeners uncritically accept "snake oil" in situations that require careful thought and analysis, they may be giving in to a desire for listening to be easy and undemanding. It may be enjoyable to listen to speakers who flatter us, tell funny stories and jokes, provide easy answers, and disparage hard work and careful thought. It is often easy to listen to those who attack and criticize the same things which we dislike, but uncritical acceptance of such speaking places the listener in a precarious position. In short, the difficulties of effective listening cannot really be overcome by seeking out easy, fun listening situations.

SITUATIONAL HABITS

Undesirable listening habits can be encouraged by conditions in the listening environment. Thus, listening can be difficult when the environment contains distractions or when the speaker's material is difficult to understand. Additionally, listening may be inhibited by distractions within the speaker.

DISTRACTIONS

In communication theory the word *noise* is frequently used to stand for anything which interferes with the communication process. Miller (1963) states that noise equals "the possibility of error." Such mistakes, according to Miller, "may occur in encoding or decoding the messages or may be introduced while the signal is in transit over the channel" (p. 7). Thus, noise could consist of interference on the part of the speaker (the encoder), interference in the environment (the channel), or interference on the part of the listener (the decoder).

If, for example, the speaker fidgets or engages in some other distracting behavior, one could say that he or she is introducing noise into the communication effect. If people are talking in the room, if the acoustics are poor, or if the seats are uncomfortable, one could conclude that there is noise in the channels of communication. If we, as listeners, are thinking about other matters, feeling physically uncomfortable, or attaching different meanings to the symbols than the speaker is, we might say that we are providing noise. And whenever we allow noise to distract us from careful, accurate listening, our effectiveness as listeners will decline.

You cannot always eliminate distractions and other forms of interference in listening situations. But if you justify *not* listening because the speaker has a poor speaking voice, uses difficult words, or exhibits annoying mannerisms you are giving in to distractions. If you excuse yourself for not hearing or understanding a message because you must strain to overcome poor acoustics or sit in an uncomfortable chair, you are using distractions as an excuse for not listening. And if you give up because you experience difficulty with the speaker's words or ideas or because you are tired and do not feel like concentrating, you are in danger of allowing interferences to inhibit your listening effort. Noise thus becomes a scapegoat for poor listening.

Realistically, no one can be expected to overcome all such problems in every situation. Sometimes the noise may become so intense that listeners cannot possibly avoid letting it adversely affect their listening efforts. The point of this discussion, however, is that one cannot let distractions or interferences become a convenient excuse for poor listening. Being distracted easily becomes a habitual response in our listening, making us feel justified for ineffective listening.

FEAR OF DIFFICULT MATERIAL

Numerous listening situations are difficult rather than easy or fun. Employees sometimes encounter such situations when required to take in-service courses in subjects they find strange and incomprehensible. Or, a person might be forced into a situation requiring him or her to work for someone who is difficult and demanding.

Such circumstances can lead to avoidance and/or rationalization. Both responses lead, as Nichols and Stevens (1957) express it, to "a diminishing downward spiral of listening ability" (p. 108). Because, as Adams and Floyd (1977) suggest, "it is unpleasant to experience failure we frequently strive to minimize its occurrence" (p. 38). Instead of facing a difficult listening situation, we practice poor listening techniques and habits, excusing ourselves because the material or situation was difficult.

Avoidance can occur in a variety of ways, even when you cannot physically avoid the situation. You can, for example, refuse to attend to the speaker. Instead of trying to listen you daydream, doodle, talk to the person next to you, and so forth. In effect, you have given up on the listening situation and refused to come to grips with it. Since it is too difficult to understand, you simply spend your time in some other way. Then, when you discover that you have indeed failed to learn or to understand, you have created a form of self-fulfilling prophecy; you *knew* it was too hard, and that absolves you of responsibility.

People also engage in a wide variety of rationalizations. As discussed earlier in this chapter, they may comfort themselves by stating that the speaker and the material were dull and uninteresting. They may also give free rein to their biases, repeatedly assuring themselves and others that the material is worthless, confusing, insulting, immoral, and so on. Another common rationalization is to blame someone else. "My adviser should never have forced me to take the class." "The department simply uses this course to get rid of people they do not like." But regardless of which rationalization is employed, the fact remains that people often fail to listen, and later on, this may prove costly.

AN OBTAINABLE GOAL

The problems discussed in this chapter are avoidable. If you make an effort to understand them, you will be in a good position to analyze your own listening habits and begin the extremely important process of becoming a more effective listener. The remaining chapters in this book are designed to help you meet that goal.

REFERENCES

Adams, W. C. and J. J. Floyd. "Failure Is Not a Four-Letter Word." *Phi Kappa Phi Journal* 57 (1977), 37–40.

Barker, L. *Listening Behavior*. Englewood Cliffs, N.J.: Prentice-Hall, 1971.

Braden, W. "The Available Means of Persuasion: What Shall We Do About the Demand for Snake Oil?" In *The Rhetoric of Our Times,* J. J. Auer, ed. New York: Appleton-Century-Crofts, 1969, 178–184.

Catania, A. C. "The Nature of Learning." In *The Study of Behavior: Learning, Motivation, Emotion and Instinct,* J. A. Nevin, ed. Glenview, Ill.: Scott, Foresman, 1973, 31–68.

Ehninger, D., B. E. Gronbeck, and A. H. Monroe. *Principles of Speech Communication.* 8th ed. Glenview, Ill.: Scott, Foresman, 1980.

Hasher, L. and R. Zacks. "Automatic and Effortful Processes in Memory." *Journal of Experimental Psychology: General* 108 (1979), 356–388.

Makay, J. J. and W. R. Brown. *The Rhetorical Dialogue: Contemporary Concepts and Cases.* Dubuque, Iowa: Wm. C. Brown, 1972.

Miller, G. A. *Language and Communication.* New York: McGraw-Hill, 1963.

Mursell, J. L. *How to Make and Break Habits.* Philadelphia: Lippincott, 1953.

Nichols, R. G. and L. A. Stevens. *Are You Listening?* New York: McGraw-Hill, 1957.

Rachlin, H. *Behavior and Learning.* San Francisco: W. H. Freeman, 1976.

Sperry Corporation. "Your Personal Listening Profile."

Stroh, C. M. *Vigilance: The Problem of Sustained Attention.* Oxford, N.Y.: Pergamon Press, 1971.

Weaver, C. H. *Human Listening: Processes and Behavior.* Indianapolis: Bobbs-Merrill, 1972.

KEY TERMS

Habits

The entertainment syndrome

Biases

Uncritical listening

Distractions

Fear of difficult material

Roles

Passive listening

EXERCISES

1. After thinking about and observing your own listening in a variety of situations, make a list of listening behaviors which you would like to eliminate or reduce. Note the kinds of situations in which these undesirable behaviors seem to be most common or troublesome.

2. In small groups discuss and list the most bothersome distractions in your classroom. Share and compare the various groups' findings.

3. With friends or class members, share your favorite daydreams which you experience during lectures. Try to discover when and how they get started.

4. Make two lists on the chalkboard: *Speaker Responsibilities* and *Listener Responsibilities*. After making these lists try to determine which items could be placed into a third list called *Shared Responsibilities*.

5. Listen as someone reads what you consider to be difficult material. After he or she tests you on the material, discuss how you felt about the material and how it affected your listening.

6. Choose a listening situation in which you feel that the topic and/or speaker is going to be dull and boring. Make an effort to listen from start to finish. Share your observations about this experience with friends, co-workers, or classmates.

3

TOWARD EFFECTIVE LISTENING HABITS

OBJECTIVES

1. To begin to inventory your listening habits.
2. To understand the general process for replacing undesirable listening habits.
3. To better understand the steps involved in becoming an effective listener.

As discussed in chapter 2, undesirable listening behaviors are frequently habitual. Skinner (1953) explains the development of habits by a process called *operant conditioning*. Essentially, this means that when a behavior is tried repeatedly and found to be positively reinforcing, it may become habitual. Generally, the reinforcement must be rewarding rather than punishing, as people will usually continue doing that which is pleasant or satisfying. The more consistently rewarding the behavior, the more a person is likely to repeat it. As the rewards continue to accompany the behavior, it becomes increasingly likely that it may become habitual.

Throughout your life you have been developing listening habits as you have learned to respond to the various messages you have heard. For the most part such habits have been formed as you were rewarded, or at least satisfied, by the results of your listening behaviors. If, for example, you have repeatedly found it more rewarding to daydream rather than to struggle with difficult material, there is a strong chance that you habitually daydream in difficult listening situations. Or, if you have felt satisfied by spending most of the time thinking about what you are going to say next rather than listening to the other person, you probably do so habitually.

The difficulties that you'll encounter in changing your undesirable listening habits will probably depend on how strongly the habits are established. This is determined by such factors as

1. how *often* a habit is rewarding

2. how *much* reward you receive from it
   and

3. how *long* you have had the habit

It is also important for you to realize that developing new, and better, habits depends on whether you see a need to change and whether you are able to receive positive rewards as a result of working toward new listening habits.

INVENTORYING YOUR LISTENING HABITS

As a first step in the development of more desirable listening habits, use the undesirable, or ineffective, listening characteristics discussed in chapter 2 as a basis for observing your own listening behaviors. In a variety of settings you can discover whether you engage in these practices, how frequently you do them, and the specific circumstances which appear to trigger them. If, for example, you catch yourself daydreaming during a lecture, a meeting, or a sermon, you can examine your attitude toward those situations. You may find that, while there is good reason to listen, the subject matter is dull and it is much easier to sit and think about something else. If you repeatedly find yourself doing this in similar situations, it is probably safe to assume that daydreaming is one of your listening habits.

Similarly, you might find that when certain subjects are discussed, or when people assume positions on issues that clash with your position or use approaches that you dislike, you think about other matters, argue (silently or vocally) with the speaker, or talk to someone sitting next to you. Again, if such behavior occurs repeatedly, and if you find it difficult to avoid such behaviors, you probably have a different bad listening habit—*listening through biases*. The crucial factor consists of your willingness to observe objectively the kinds of practices you engage in during various types of listening situations.

Some habits relate to listening behavior but cannot be observed during listening situations *per se*. One student, for example, indicated that whenever she knew that a classroom lecture would cover difficult material, she managed to convince herself that she was too ill to attend class. This is clearly an example of fear of difficult material and represents a habitual avoidance response to such listening situations.

You should also weigh the various types of listening situations that you encounter. You will probably discover that undesirable listening habits apply to some situations but not to others. In lecture settings, for example, you may find that the desire to talk rather than listen is not a problem. Yet in interpersonal, conversational situations, you may notice that people repeatedly fail to listen because they are constantly looking for the opportunity to do the talking. Or you might discover that when listening to authority figures you are less able to set aside your biases than when listening to your peers or colleagues.

One possible method for taking inventory of your listening habits is suggested by Wolvin and Coakley in their discussion of types of *listening purposes*. They indicate that people listen for *appreciation*, for *discrimination*, for *comprehension*, for *therapy*, and for *criticism* or *evaluation* (1979, pp. 7–13). Appreciation listening occurs when you are seeking enjoyment or pleasure. Discriminative listening refers to listening in which you are trying to interpret symbols accurately and in which you want to distinguish between symbols correctly. In comprehensive listening you are striving to understand a message accurately: you want to *learn* from the listening experience. Therapeutic listening applies to less formal situations in which you allow another person to do most of the talking while you attempt to understand and to empathize. Critical listening involves those situations in which you want to judge and respond to messages. After considering such listening purposes, make an effort to evaluate your strengths and weaknesses in those areas.

ELIMINATING UNDESIRABLE HABITS

In this section we will explore three steps that can be employed in the process of eliminating undesirable habits and substituting habits more conducive to effective listening. The three steps are (1) *recognition,* (2) *refusal,* and (3) *replacement.*

RECOGNITION

Once you are aware of your undesirable listening habits and the situations in which they typically occur, you are in a position to begin the process of changing them. Keeping in mind the fact that such habits have probably developed over a period of time, you need to realize that doing away with them is anything but an easy task. Such habits are usually comfortable, easy to drift into, and largely unconscious. Being aware of them is not enough. You must learn to "catch yourself in the act." If, for example, you are attending a business meeting and begin to daydream or rethink some problem, you have to *recognize* that you are doing it. In a sense, this means that you must make a continuous effort to monitor your own listening behavior.

As an example of such monitoring, consider the student who leaves home to attend college in another state. This student discovers that his or her speech patterns sound strange and, at times, inappropriate to others in the new environment. At first the student may be totally unaware of these differences but soon realizes that people react with amusement, or even disdain. Eventually, then, this student becomes aware of the differences and learns, as a result of study and/or instruction, what constitutes "acceptable" grammar. This does not mean, however, that our student will stop using incorrect or unacceptable grammar immediately. Since he or she is striving to overcome strongly established grammatical patterns, the tendency to use them will persist. Thus he or she must strive to recognize each use of an old construction. One might argue at this point that with enough exposure over time to "correct" usage, the old habits will disappear effortlessly. Nevertheless, if the student wants to initiate change as soon as possible, he or she must learn to recognize the use of undesirable grammar as it occurs. We might note, also, that even though grammar might improve with exposure to correct use, there is no such process in listening. The tendency is, as we have seen, for undesirable habits to persist and strengthen over time.

While we might consider other significant differences between correcting grammar and listening improvement, the concept of recognition as a first step in habit modification applies to either situation. Any attempt to replace undesirable listening habits will almost certainly fail unless the individual cultivates the desire and the ability to recognize the actual functioning of such habits as they occur in various listening situations.

REFUSAL

As important as it is to recognize those times in which you fall into poor listening habits, the second step in habit modification is equally important—and perhaps more difficult. This step means, essentially, that you force yourself not to tolerate bad listening when you recognize it in your listening activities. Because habitual behavior is ingrained and generally comfortable, you have to learn to fight against it repeatedly even when you are fully aware that it is present. Anyone who has developed the unfortunate habit of cigarette smoking knows very well how true this is. If a person tries to stop smoking it is extremely easy to fail, regardless of determination and desire to quit. Typically the desire to smoke is associated with various situations in which the smoker tends to "light up" automatically. While those vary from person to person, some of the common situations might be social settings, times of boredom, the morning cup of coffee, and times of tension and stress. During the process of quitting, the smoker may be quite conscious of the desire to give in at such times. He or she may succeed in holding out, only to have the urge to smoke creep up again and again. Getting through such moments successfully probably represents the greatest difficulty for one who attempts to give up smoking. They do not happen once or twice; they occur repeatedly. Success depends on winning battle after battle.

In an important sense the same problem confronts those who are trying to improve as listeners. You know very well that biased listening is undesirable. You recognize it in your own listening behavior repeatedly. But in spite of that, it is easy to do when the speaker says something you disagree with. As the smoker may fight off the urge to smoke only to have it creep up again and again, the listener might fight off the temptation to argue with the speaker one minute only to give in to it a few minutes later. The old habit is

---

Listening Lab

System for Improving Listening Habits

* Review your listening inventory
* Recognize your undesirable listening habits
* Refuse to tolerate undesirable habits
* Replace undesirable habits with effective ones

always the easier way to go in listening. Refusal means, then, that you refuse to give in to undesirable habits again and again. It is easy to say but very hard to do. Yet listening improvement and its attendant benefits depend on it.

REPLACEMENT

The third step involved in changing habits emerges naturally from refusal. Each time you refuse to continue engaging in an undesirable habit you have won a victory of sorts over that habit. But that alone is not enough. Through a gradual process, you need to begin replacing the undesirable habit with behavior that will be conducive to effective listening. In essence, replacement calls for the development of new habits, and that takes time.

In the remaining chapters of this book we will examine *specific* ways to develop better listening habits.

BEGINNING RULES FOR BETTER LISTENING

Since listening appears to involve a complex of behaviors rather than a single, easily identifiable act, it is difficult, if not impossible, to make a comprehensive list of behaviors that one can substitute for undesirable listening habits. This is not to say, however, that various lists are not available. They may prove useful as a starting point for those who want to have a general idea of the kinds of behaviors that should replace bad habits.

The Sperry Corporation provides a list, for example, which contrasts "The Bad Listener" with "The Good Listener." (See table 3.1.) That list offers the following suggestions: (1) Whereas the bad listener "tunes out dry subjects," the good listener finds opportunity in any situation by asking "what's in it for me?" (2) The bad listener "tunes out" poor delivery, while the effective listener focuses on content and "skips over delivery errors." (3) Bad listeners are ready to argue; good listeners avoid judging "until comprehension [is] complete." (4) Ineffective listeners listen for "facts," but effective listeners watch for "central themes." (5) Bad listeners take too many notes, "using only one system"; good listeners take "fewer notes," using a variety of note-taking methods. (6) The poor listener puts little energy into listening and often fakes attention, while the good listener "works hard," and shows an "active body state." (7) The bad listener is easily distracted, but the good listener "avoids distractions, tolerates bad habits [in the speaker]," and "knows how to concentrate." (8) When material is difficult, poor listeners resist listening, while good listeners use "heavier material as exercise for the mind." (9) Ineffective listeners react to "emotional words," but effective listeners interpret them without getting "hung up." (10) Bad listeners daydream; the good listener "challenges, anticipates, mentally summarizes, weighs the evidence, listens between the lines to tone of voice" (p. 6).

In summary, the central point of this chapter revolves around the process of establishing positive and effective behaviors *in the place of* listening habits which reduce your capacity to attend to, understand, analyze, evaluate, and ultimately respond intelligently to all types of messages. Replacement means, in a sense, that you learn to listen as well in difficult situations as you do when you are highly motivated and interested. I firmly believe that you have the ability to listen effectively; hopefully, the personal rewards will make it worthwhile for you to change your listening habits.

PERSONAL REWARDS

At this point you might conclude that, on balance, listening improvement through habit modification is a bleak and joyless business. One could conclude that listening improvement is too much trouble and not really worth the effort. After all, you have been living your life this far without falling apart over the fact that you may not be an outstanding listener. However, even though you can expect to suffer setbacks, and even though you may progress slowly and in small degrees, the progress can prove rewarding. When you discover that you engage in poor listening habits less frequently, or

Figure 3.1   10 keys to effective listening

These keys are a positive guideline to better listening. In fact, they're at the heart of developing better listening habits that could last a lifetime.

10 Keys to Effective Listening	The Bad Listener	The Good Listener
1. Find areas of interest	Tunes out dry subjects	Opportunizes; asks ''what's in it for me?''
2. Judge content, not delivery	Tunes out if delivery is poor	Judges content, skips over delivery errors
3. Hold your fire	Tends to enter into argument	Doesn't judge until comprehension complete
4. Listen for ideas	Listens for facts	Listens for central themes
5. Be flexible	Takes intensive notes using only one system	Takes fewer notes. Uses 4–5 different systems, depending on speaker
6. Work at listening	Shows no energy output Attention is faked	Works hard, exhibits active body state
7. Resist distractions	Distracted easily	Fights or avoids distractions, tolerates bad habits, knows how to concentrate
8. Exercise your mind	Resists difficult expository material; seeks light, recreational material	Uses heavier material as exercise for the mind
9. Keep your mind open	Reacts to emotional words	Interprets color words; does not get hung up on them
10. Capitalize on fact that *thought* is *faster* than speech.	Tends to daydream with slow speakers	Challenges, anticipates, mentally summarizes, weighs the evidence, listens between the lines to tone of voice

This material was prepared by Dr. Lyman K. Steil, President of Communication Development, Inc., St. Paul, Minnesota for the Sperry Corporation. Reprinted by permission of Dr. Steil and the Sperry Corporation.

that you catch yourself while doing them and then put them aside, such discoveries will encourage you to try even harder to improve.

In addition, you can expect to realize *specific* results from whatever progress you make. You should actually get more out of lectures, which is likely to show up when you are taking exams. Listening situations which formerly seemed hopelessly dull and uninteresting will very likely take on some significance for you that you would otherwise fail to grasp. You might begin to notice positive differences in the way you relate to others and in their responses to you socially and interpersonally. As these kinds of results occur, it is difficult to imagine that you will regret working on changing your listening habits.

A second reward will be your discovery of the richness of effective listening. Students in listening classes each term repeatedly express their surprise at discovering how complicated and challenging listening is. On student evaluations of the course they consistently convey their appreciation for this discovery and remark that it has totally changed their attitudes toward the role of the listener in the communication process. When one struggles to improve in a challenging activity, appreciation for that activity appears to grow out of the struggle. To illustrate this point, most of us have probably watched professional golf tournaments on television. After a while one can get a highly distorted view of the difficulty of that sport and of the skills required to play it well. Although announcers, commentators, and even the golfers themselves may refer to "poor shots," "bad putts," and "bad rounds," their standards of judgment are based on the abilities of professionals who are all excellent players. Thus, to non-golfers, the game may seem much easier than it actually is. If you play the game yourself you will probably discover that it is difficult and challenging. By way of comparison, it seems highly unlikely that anyone who has struggled to understand the listening process and to replace bad habits with good ones will conclude that listening is easy or that anyone can do it well without trying.

Perhaps of greatest importance, however, is the possibility that striving to improve as listeners will strengthen your self-concept. This can be observed from a variety of perspectives. First, it is a rare person who does not feel good about himself or herself as a result of meeting difficult challenges successfully. Failures that occurred along the way only sweeten the feeling of achievement. Second, if you become a better listener by succeeding at the difficult task of changing long-established habits, there is every reason to believe that you can tackle other challenges successfully. Third, if you discover improvement in your attitudes toward other people and enjoy the reinforcement of discovering that they react more positively toward you as you listen effectively to them, your sense of self-worth is bound to strengthen considerably.

In the remaining chapters of this book we will discuss specific behaviors that you can use to replace your undesirable listening habits. Emphasizing how to overcome major barriers to effective listening, we will examine those aspects of the communication process that are the listener's responsibility. This discussion will be applied to situations in which you function as listeners in an audience as well as to those situations in which you are communicating face-to-face in interactional settings.

REFERENCES

Skinner, B. F. *Science and Human Behavior.* New York: Macmillan, 1953.
Sperry Corporation. "Your Listening Profile."
Wolvin, A. D. and C. G. Coakley. *Listening Instruction.* Urbana, Ill.: ERIC Clearinghouse on Reading and Communication Skills, 1979.

KEY TERMS

Recognition

Refusal

Replacement

Inventory

Appreciative listening

Discriminative listening

Comprehensive listening

Therapeutic listening

Critical listening

EXERCISES

1. Make an inventory of your undesirable listening habits. Consult friends, relatives, and teachers for examples and suggestions. Share and discuss your inventories in small groups.

2. Explore ways in which habits are established, how they are helpful, and how they are detrimental to you.

3. Describe successes and failures that you encountered in attempting to change what you consider to be your worst listening habit.

4. Make a list of personal benefits which you think could result from improved listening. Share your list with others, and seek their responses.

5. Choose a listening situation in which you can function as an observer. Take notes on the kinds of listening behaviors that take place among the audience members.

CHAPTER

4

OVERCOMING BARRIERS TO ATTENTION

OBJECTIVES

1. To understand the importance of attention in listening.
2. To identify factors which affect attention adversely.
3. To begin the process of overcoming barriers to attention in your listening.

C onsider the following situation. Sara and Joe meet for lunch in a crowded restaurant. Sara is trying to tell Joe about a problem at work, but Joe is busy observing a dispute between another customer and a waiter. Even though Joe is aware of Sara and the sound of her voice, he is paying little attention to what she is saying. When she asks him a question he is startled into the realization that at best he has only a vague idea of what she said. Sara feels frustrated and says, "You didn't hear a word I said." Actually, Joe did hear Sara's voice; the problem is that he was not paying attention.

Since you cannot attend to all the stimuli surrounding you, you must select what you will attend to and what you will not. According to Stroh (1971), there are two factors involved in the selection process: one must "focus" and "maintain attention" (p. 1). You thus *choose* to concentrate on something that you wish to perceive or understand. Attending to something means that you *focus on it* and *attempt to sustain the focus*. As various auditory stimuli reach your ears, attention results from the decisions you make in selecting what you will focus upon. In contrast, stimuli that you choose to ignore will not be attended to, or focused on.

THE IMPORTANCE OF ATTENTION

If you want to improve as a listener, it is important to realize that decisions about what you will pay attention to in listening situations go a long way in determining how well you will understand, evaluate, and respond. In listening, you will hear numerous messages and be exposed to a variety of competing stimuli in the listening environment. You will not stop hearing other messages or various environmental distractions. In the process of choosing the messages you will focus upon, you may be affected by unchosen stimuli at the same time you attend to the selected messages (see Treisman, 1969, and Tyson, 1982). For the most part, however, your attitudes, values, past experiences, and motivations will determine what you attend to and how fully you do so (see Norman, 1968).

And even when you succeed in focusing your attention on a spoken message, competing stimuli will *continue to* intrude on your attention. When those competing stimuli succeed in dividing your attention, your ability to understand and to recall the message you have heard will be adversely affected (Norman, 1969). You have probably experienced this in a variety of situations. Recall, for example, times in which you were embarrassed because you were asked to respond to something someone said and had only a vague idea of what it was—because you were concentrating on something else.

It requires considerable effort to attend to a message. Yet anyone who wants to listen more effectively must realize this fact and strive, through motivation and habit modification, to work hard to pay close attention when listening to others. Essentially, it is a matter, not of attending better, but of deciding what to focus your attention on in listening situations.

FACTORS AFFECTING ATTENTION

Factors which affect your attention may be considered from two perspectives. First, attention may be affected by factors external to the listener, such as the message or the speaker. Second, your attention may be affected by factors within you, the listener.

EXTERNAL FACTORS

You will probably agree that some things seem inherently interesting, while others fail to catch your attention. Three characteristics help to explain why you pay attention to some objects and not to others—*variety, novelty,* and *intensity*. Variety helps to attract and sustain attention. For that reason, curves are intentionally placed in interstate highways as a means of helping people to pay attention to their driving. The variety helps to keep them alert. And when you are studying, concentration and attention can be enhanced by alternating subjects rather than studying each subject for long periods of time. The unusual, the novel, attracts more attention than the commonplace, ordinary object. In a televised football game the unusual play is far more likely to be replayed than the ordinary play. Finally, intensity refers to factors which stand out sufficiently to attract attention. The referee's whistle is shrill in order to insure that the players will pay attention to it. If your alarm clock produced a soft, soothing sound it would not serve its purpose.

Such factors probably contribute to the common tendency to expect speakers and their messages to command attention before listeners are willing to pay much attention to them. As you may recall, this expectation relates to the problem known as the entertainment syndrome.

LISTENER FACTORS

Attention is also affected by the attitudes and expectations within the listener. You may realize that your willingness to pay attention to others is affected by your needs, interests, and prior expectations (see Colburn and Weinberg, 1976, pp. 2–3). Thus, if you are interested in a subject you will probably pay more attention than if you feel that it is of no value or importance. You may find it easier to pay attention to a speaker you consider interesting or attractive than to one who strikes you as dull or unattractive. Similarly, if you are expecting one type of discussion and hear another, your attention may wane.

While these listener characteristics are understandable, it is important to realize that they can serve as barriers to effective listening, especially when they lead you to stop listening prior to understanding.

THE DAYDREAMING BARRIER

As listeners you must continuously make choices. When you decide that the material is not interesting enough, is too difficult or taxing, or that various distractions are making it too difficult to listen, you always have alternative behaviors available. Quite often you may choose a less difficult and more agreeable behavior (Jung, 1978, p. 266). Daydreaming is frequently one such alternative. It requires little effort. You can be physically present in the listening situation, but mentally far removed. So you sit in a classroom and think about what you did last weekend. Or you think about an exciting activity which is coming up in the near future. With very little effort you can imagine almost any past, present, or future event without leaving your seat. Daydreaming thus provides an alternative to listening.

The advantages of daydreaming are numerous, making it a frequently self-reinforcing behavior. It is private. No one knows for sure if and when you are doing it. One can appear at full attention, hanging on the speaker's words, while actually thinking about something else. It is also an activity which disturbs no one else. The speaker need not be distracted; others are in no way prevented from listening. No wonder you find yourself repeatedly drifting into a good daydream when you should be involved in the much more demanding process of listening.

Quite simply, daydreaming creates attention problems. While it is not impossible to do two or more things at the same time, it is difficult "to handle more than a critical amount of information in a given time" (Broadbent, 1958, pp. 34–35). You may be able to drive a car and think about a problem at work, but as you pay more attention to the problem and less attention to driving the car, you may find yourself failing to attend to a stop sign. Similarly, while listening you may "hear" the speaker and think about something else, but one of these two behaviors may lose out. As you get farther into the daydream you attend to less and less of the speaker's message (Broadbent, 1958, p. 68). The more intense the daydream, the less you may attend to the message.

You can try to keep in mind the various costly and embarrassing consequences of daydreaming as a starting point or motivation for improvement. Then you can apply the three steps of habit modification (recognition, refusal, and replacement). First, you have to catch yourself in the act of daydreaming. You have to do this repeatedly and over time. Catching yourself once in a while will have little impact on a habitual behavior. Second, every time you catch yourself daydreaming, bring it to an immediate halt and return to concentrating on the speaker and the message. This step, too, has to be done repeatedly. Third, you need to do something constructive in place of daydreaming. For example: concentrate on the speaker and the message; take advantage of the extra time that thinking provides over speaking; relate one part of the message to another; summarize what you have already heard; think of questions you might ask; and provide feedback to the speaker. These are positive listening behaviors which you can use *in place of* daydreaming.

Keep in mind that replacing the daydreams with *constructive* behavior is your goal. If you merely substitute one bad habit for another, you will not have made much progress. Drawing pictures, talking to the person next to you, or taking a nap do not constitute constructive alternatives to daydreaming. One must continuously fight against it, and, at the same time, get involved in the business of concentrating on speaker and message. Daydreaming is a habit—easy to do and difficult to avoid. Your efforts to overcome it will pay rich dividends in improved listening.

THE NOISE BARRIER

A major reason for inadequate attention relates directly to the quantity of stimuli that confronts each of us during every listening effort. Whenever stimuli other than the speaker and message win out, you run the risk of not attending to the message. Unfortunately, the kinds of distractions possible during listening situations are virtually unlimited. Everyone who wants to become a better listener must be willing to come to grips with this problem.

ENVIRONMENTAL NOISE

Some noise comes from the environment. If people are walking and talking outside of the room in which you are trying to listen, your attention may be drawn away from the speaker. If those around you are talking, dropping items, or making noises you may be distracted from listening. In a room which is far too hot or cold, you may find yourself having trouble concentrating on the speaker. It may be, too, that other interesting stimuli in the environment may successfully vie for your attention. These may include pictures on the wall, activities outside the room, or an attractive person nearby. The point is that any number of environmental factors can draw you away from attending to a message to the extent that you fail to attend to what the speaker is saying.

SELF-GENERATED NOISE

Another category of distractions results from internal factors, or what we might refer to as *self-generated* distractions. These kinds of distractions result from factors too numerous to discuss individually. Our purpose should be served, however, by discussing enough of these distractions to clarify the idea that we often distract ourselves. If, for example, you are suffering from some physical discomfort, such as a headache or stomachache, you will have difficulty paying attention to the speaker. Personal problems may also qualify as a form of distraction that inhibits our attention to the message. Fear of difficult material, particularly in relation to the fear of failure, may distract you from effective listening. Internal distractions can also lead to distraction by environmental factors, to "thinking of other things, . . . looking out the window, and concentrating on different objects or pieces of equipment in the room" (Kleinke, 1978, p. 71).

Another form of self-generated noise results from the tendency to talk rather than listen (see chapter 2). When you are

---

Listening Lab

Improving Your Ability to Pay Attention

* Resist the temptation to daydream
* Reduce environmental distraction
* Ignore internal (self-generated) distractions
* Refuse to be distracted by speaker appearance and mannerisms
* Repeatedly remind yourself to focus on the message

concentrating on what you are going to say or how you will respond to the speaker, your attention may be diverted from the speaker and his or her message.

SPEAKER NOISE

A third type of distraction can come from the speaker. Nervous mannerisms, clothing, voice quality, nonfluent delivery, lack of eye contact, physical appearance, and similar factors frequently serve to distract attention away from the message. Before they realize it, listeners drift into a pattern of paying more attention to the speaker's appearance and/or behaviors than what he or she actually says.

REMOVING DISTRACTIONS

Learning to overcome the problem of distractions is no easy task. Realistically, it might be impossible. After all, there are always going to be distractions in any listening situation, and no one can develop powers of concentration sufficient to enable him or her to block them out. In fact, some distractions simply cannot be overcome. If someone is operating a jackhammer outside the room, for example, there is no way to remain unaffected. If the temperature in a room is 100 degrees, how can you possibly avoid being distracted? But even if you agree that there is truth to these statements, you need to consider what can be done to minimize the interference of noise.

In some instances you can solve the problem of noise quite easily through minor adjustments. If distractions are winning the battle for your attention because the speaker is speaking too softly, under most circumstances you can move closer, or request the speaker to speak louder. In this way, you have found a way to adjust. Sometimes closing a window or door will be sufficient to shut out distracting sounds. Perhaps opening a door or window will reduce distractions such as excessive heat or stuffiness in the room.

At other times you may have to remove the distraction altogether before it is possible to concentrate on hearing the speaker. It might be necessary, for example, to change rooms. Other possibilities include such remedies as replacing a blinking fluorescent light, asking noisy people to hold it down or even asking them to leave the room, requesting workmen to come back later, erasing material from the chalkboard, providing more comfortable seating, and so forth. While these remedies may seem too obvious even to mention, it is surprising how often people tolerate distractions in spite of the fact that they could easily overcome them. Once again, the important factor may be how motivated you are to listen effectively. If you really feel that it is important to listen, you will not tolerate distractions that could just as easily be lessened or eliminated.

LISTENING OVER NOISE

Unfortunately, however, the problem of distractions cannot always be handled by making simple changes in the environment. One reason for this is that the problem of distractions is not simply environmental. As discussed earlier, the problem frequently lies within us—the listeners. Murch (1973) indicates that noise, "in the sense of that which interferes or blocks out" is "a property of the sensory system." His examples include "fatigue, motivation, stimulus adaptation, changes in attention, and spontaneous, random neural activity within the sensory system" (p. 19). This suggests that people have the capacity to ignore or close out irrelevant sounds. Studies by Cherry (1953) and Moray (1959) indicate that people who engage in this behavior have the capacity to pay some attention to the sounds that are essentially being ignored. If some relevant sound occurs, such as the speaking of the person's name, he or she has the capacity to switch over to the previously "ignored" source. This ability means, for example, that you can stop attending to the person who is talking and "listen in" on some other conversation that is going on around you.

As a practical illustration, assume that you are involved in a conversation with a friend in the coffee room at work. Other conversations are taking place at the same time, but as your friend speaks you block out those surrounding conversations. However, you suddenly realize that in one of the conversations someone is talking about a comment you made in a recent meeting. As you hear your name mentioned you switch over to that conversation, ignoring what your friend is saying.

It would be unlikely that you could later recount much of what your friend said after you switched your attention. At best, you caught only bits and pieces of the ignored message. The same is true of the nearby conversation prior to the time that you switched your attention to it.

In spite of the fact that you do not *entirely* ignore what you block out, a major problem in listening occurs when you concentrate on stimuli other than the speaker. While you may technically receive the sound of the speaker's voice and have some limited awareness of what the speaker is saying, it requires a considerable stretch of the imagination to conclude that you are listening to the speaker in any practical sense.

The important factor which emerges from the above statements is that we do not have to have perfect conditions in order to pay attention to messages. On the contrary, we have at our disposal a variety of methods for adjusting to distractions rather than giving in to them. Moore (1977) tells us, in his *Introduction to the Psychology of Hearing,* that "speech intelligibility is relatively little affected by severe corrupting influences." He goes on to indicate that "speech can be accurately understood in the presence of huge amounts of background noise. . . ." (p. 239). Thus, no unavoidable reason exists for us to have to give in to distractions. Conditions do not *have* to be free of distractions.

Moore's discussion suggests that you must learn to concentrate on the message by first blocking out *competing stimuli.* While this feat is not easy, it can be achieved. Its success rests primarily with your motivation. Second, you should attempt to apply the three parts of habit modification: try to be aware of the times in which you are giving in to the distractions, refuse to tolerate them, and return to attending to the speaker.

COMPRESSED SPEECH

There are recent indications that attention, as well as memory and comprehension, can be enhanced through a technique known as compressed speech. Compressed speech consists of electronically speeding up oral presentations without affecting intelligibility

(Gerber, 1968). This technique rests on the assumption that listeners will make more effective use of their time if they have less time to waste. With too much time a listener can drift away from a message and attend to competing stimuli. As Nichols (1969) points out, the difference "between thought speed and speech speed breeds false feelings of security and mental tangents" (p. 479).

Apparently people can attend to and comprehend speech presented considerably faster than the normal speaking rate. Orr (1968) says that listeners can handle rates of 275–300 words per minute without any adverse effect on retention (p. 289). Similarly, Olsen (1979) places the optimal rate at 250–325 words per minute (p. 67). Barabasz (1968) found that lectures can be presented at rates which reduce "presentation time" by "one-third, without any significant loss in recall and retention" (p. 287). And Woodcock and Clark concluded that listeners can retain material presented at 228–328 words per minute (Woodcock and Clark, 1968).

Some scholars are enthused over possible uses for compressed speech in listening, particularly in business, schools, mass media advertising, law enforcement, and hospitals (Wolvin and Coakley, 1982, pp. 89–90).

As promising as this technique may be, it is not a panacea for listeners. It must be utilized under conditions conducive to using electronic devices. In the majority of daily communication settings this is not the case. Further, compressed speech does not guarantee interest and attention (Weaver, 1972, p. 148). Also, while compressed speech may not hinder intelligibility, retention, and comprehension, it does not necessarily enhance these skills. The major advantage seems to consist in saving time for listeners and speakers. By reducing the amount of time needed to convey a message, compressed speech could reduce the time available for inattention.

There are, however, at least two ways in which your listening may be affected by the research findings relative to compressed speech. First, you can use such information to remind yourself that rapid delivery is not necessarily a valid excuse for ineffective listening. As long as a speaker's rate is intelligible, there is apparently no good reason why you cannot successfully attend to and comprehend the message. Second, if compressed speech is utilized in mass media advertising, you may eventually be exposed to this technique on a daily basis. Again, your ability to attend to and comprehend such messages should be essentially unaffected.

REFERENCES

Barabasz, A. F. "A Study of Recall and Retention of Accelerated Lecture Presentation." *The Journal of Communication* 18 (1968), 283–287.

Broadbent, D. E. *Perception and Communication.* London: Pergamon, 1958.

Cherry, C. "Some Experiments on the Recognition of Speech, with One and Two Ears." *Journal of the Acoustical Society of America* 25 (1953), 975–979.

Colburn, C. W. and S. B. Weinberg. *An Orientation to Listening and Audience Analysis.* Chicago: Science Research Associates, 1976.

Gerber, S. E. "Dichotic and Diotic Presentation of Speeded Speech." *The Journal of Communication* 18 (1968), 272–282.

Jung, J. *Understanding Human Motivation.* New York: Macmillan, 1978.

Kleinke, C. L. *Self-Perception.* San Francisco: W. H. Freeman, 1978.

Moore, B. C. J. *Introduction to the Psychology of Hearing.* Baltimore: University Park Press, 1977.

Moray, N. "Attention in Dichotic Listening: Affective Cues and the Influence of Instruction." *Quarterly Journal of Experimental Psychology* 11 (1959), 56–60.

Murch, G. *Visual and Auditory Perception.* Indianapolis: Bobbs-Merrill, 1973.

Nichols, R. G. "Listening Is a 10-Part Skill." In *Readings in Interpersonal and Organizational Communication.* R. C. Huseman et al., eds. Boston: Holbrook Press, 1969, 472–479.

Norman, D. A. "Toward a Theory of Memory and Attention." *Psychological Review* 75 (1968), 522–536.

Norman, D. A. "Memory While Shadowing." *Quarterly Journal of Experimental Psychology* 21 (1969), 85–93.

Olsen, L. "Technology-Humanized: The Rate-Controlled Tape Recorder." *Media and Methods* 15 (1979), 67.

Orr, D. B. "Time Compressed Speech—A Perspective." *The Journal of Communication* 18 (1968), 288–292.

Stroh, C. M. *Vigilance: The Problem of Sustained Attention.* Oxford, N.Y.: Pergamon Press, 1971.

Treisman, A. M. "Strategies and Models of Selective Attention." *Psychological Review* 76 (1969), 282–299.

Tyson, P. D. "A General Systems Theory Approach to Consciousness, Attention, and Mediation." *Psychological Record* 32 (1982), 491–500.

Weaver, C. H. *Human Listening: Processes and Behavior.* Indianapolis: Bobbs-Merrill, 1972.

Wolvin, A. D. and C. G. Coakley. *Listening*. Dubuque, Iowa: Wm. C. Brown, 1982.

Woodcock, R. W. and C. R. Clark. "Comprehension of a Narrative Passage by Elementary School Children as a Function of Listening Rate, Retention Period, and I.Q." *The Journal of Communication* 18 (1968), 259–271.

KEY TERMS

Attention

Distractions

Noise

Focusing

Maintaining

Barriers to attention

Variety

Novelty

Intensity

Compressed speech

EXERCISES

1. Listen as someone reads informative material. Select three people and assign them the task of creating distractions during the reading. The distractions could consist of talking to others; dropping books, pens, purses, etc.; getting up and walking around the room; or creating a disturbance in the hall immediately outside the room.

A. Take a test over the material. Then listen to the material without the distractions.
B. Have the reader explain how the distractions affected his or her ability to present the material clearly and effectively.

2. Choose three different listening situations, each of which you find difficult and/or uninteresting. As you listen, make a concentrated effort to focus your attention on the speaker and the message. Briefly describe the listening situations and the success (or lack of it) that you experienced in your effort to attend to the speaker.

3. In small groups of approximately five persons, discuss distractions and potential distractions which can be found in your classroom. Have a member of each group report the findings to the class. Discuss ways to eliminate or minimize the distractions.

4. One day in all of your classes make a check mark each time you catch yourself daydreaming, giving in to distractions, worrying or thinking about personal matters, or listening with your biases. See how long you can go without engaging in these ineffective listening behaviors as the day progresses. Share and compare your results with others. Repeat this exercise a week or two later and see if you have improved.

5. Select a listening situation in your community. Acting as an observer, watch the behaviors of the audience members. Discuss your findings with people in your class or group.

6. Take control of your listening situation in a classroom or meeting room. Make a conscious effort to remove or reduce distractions. Perhaps you can remove material from the chalkboard, adjust the lighting, move furniture, etc. Observe the results of your efforts.

C H A P T E R

5

UNDERSTANDING NONVERBAL MESSAGES

OBJECTIVES

1. *To understand how nonverbal communication applies to our understanding of messages.*
2. *To understand the seven types of nonverbal communication.*
3. *To understand better the common problems that interfere with an accurate interpretation of nonverbal messages.*
4. *To follow the five suggestions for understanding nonverbal communication.*

I n oral communication, verbal messages hardly ever occur in isolation. Instead, they are accompanied by nonverbal messages which "repeat, contradict, substitute, complement, accent, or regulate verbal communication" (Knapp, 1978, p. 38). Some nonverbal messages are conveyed through the voice, while others are conveyed through such channels as gestures, facial expressions, body movement, use of space, and touch.

By viewing nonverbal communication as "an inseparable part of the total communication process" (Knapp, 1978, p. 38), effective listeners will strive to understand nonverbal messages in conjunction with verbal messages.

As a simple illustration, assume that you have a friend who is an excellent bowler. You are counting on this person to be the mainstay of your bowling team and casually mention that it is almost time to register the team for league competition. Your friend replies that he or she is tired of bowling and is no longer interested in being on the team, but winks as he or she speaks. If you ignore this speaker's nonverbal message, an accurate understanding of the verbal message will hardly be possible.

TYPES OF NONVERBAL COMMUNICATION

In your efforts to understand the role of nonverbal communication in the listening process, you need to be aware of the wide variety of ways in which speakers convey messages nonverbally.

Knapp (1980) divides the ways in which we communicate nonverbally into seven categories:

1. Body motion or kinesic behavior

2. Physical characteristics

3. Touching behavior

4. Paralanguage

5. Proxemics

6. Artifacts

7. Environmental factors (pp. 4–11)

BODY MOTION OR KINESIC BEHAVIOR

This category includes such physical actions as gestures, facial expressions, eye contact, posture, and movements of the limbs. As Knapp (1980) indicates, some physical actions convey feelings, and others are used to communicate "personality traits or attitudes" (p. 4). Thus, a speaker might express anger by pounding his or her fist on a table. A friend who is attempting to hide something from you might avoid eye contact and look down and away from you. A person who disagrees with you may shake his or her head negatively. Someone who is worried may frown, narrow the eyes, and place a hand on his or her forehead. Or, someone who is excited and enthused may smile, lean forward, and open his or her eyes widely. In short, physical actions express numerous cues about people's attitudes and feelings.

PHYSICAL CHARACTERISTICS

Unlike body action, physical characteristics do not change as a result of physical action. Knapp (1980) suggests that physical characteristics include "physique or body shape, general attractiveness, body or breath odors, height, weight, hair, and skin color or tone" (p. 9). Although listeners sometimes make judgments about speakers and their messages on the basis of such characteristics, it is important for you to remember that such judgments are usually unfair. They "reveal more about those who make the judgments than about those being judged" (Wood, 1982, p. 99). Also, keep in mind that physical characteristics "have no intrinsic meanings or values . . . ." Actually, "whatever meanings we associate with particular physical characteristics derive from our interpretations—a point worth remembering" (Wood, 1982, p. 99).

As an illustration, assume that you are attending a meeting with a guest speaker. Prior to the presentation you note that the speaker is short, overweight, and generally unattractive. Your attitudes toward these physical characteristics might lead you to decide that the speaker's message will be of little or no value, thus creating a negative mental set which will affect the way you interpret his or her message.

TOUCHING BEHAVIOR

Although touching is a physical behavior, it is often categorized as a separate nonverbal behavior (Knapp, 1980, p. 9). Through touch, "the most basic forms of interpersonal attitude can be communicated." And, "to a more limited extent," touch also expresses "emotional states" (Argyle, 1975, p. 286). As nonverbal communication, touch may express love, sympathy, support, anger, friendship, physical attraction, and so on. Argyle (1975) classifies touching behaviors in Western culture as *patting* (head, back); *slapping* (face, hand, bottom); *punching* (face, chest); *pinching* (cheek); *stroking* (hair, face, upper body, knee); *shaking* (hands); *kissing* (mouth, cheek, breasts, hand, foot); *licking* (face); *holding* (hand, arm, knee); *guiding* (hand, arm); *embracing* (shoulder, body); *linking* (arms); *laying on* (hands); *kicking* (bottom); *grooming* (hair, face); and *tickling* (anywhere) (1975, p. 287).

Such behaviors tend to reinforce and substitute for verbal communication. If, for example, a friend were attempting to support you during a time of frustration or disappointment, he or she might touch your arm or shoulder as a means of reinforcing words of encouragement, or as a means of silently indicating support and sympathy.

PARALANGUAGE

Mehrabian (1981) and other experts in nonverbal communication acknowledge the difference between the actual verbalizing of messages and aspects of the voice which convey emotions, attitudes, shades of meaning, and so on. Thus, paralanguage "deals with how something is said and not what is said" (Knapp, 1980, p. 9). For example, the word *no* can be spoken in such a way as to express surprise, uncertainty, disbelief, anger, joy, boredom, and so forth. Imagine a situation in which you ask someone whether he or she is angry, and that individual says "No" in a tone of voice that indicates he or she is quite angry. Because you have attended to the nonverbal message, you can more accurately interpret the speaker's verbal statement. By attending to paralanguage, listeners can thus attempt to understand speakers' personality traits, emotions, and attitudes (see Harper, Wiens, and Matarazzo, 1978, pp. 26–38).

PROXEMICS

Proxemics is a term for the ways in which people use and respond to others' use of space. It concerns such factors as the distance between and among people, seating arrangements, the manipulation of height relative to people and objects, movement within physical settings, and control of physical settings. As nonverbal communication, proxemics relates to interpersonal attitudes such as attraction, repulsion, power, and status (see Argyle, 1975, pp. 300–309).

Consider two sets of circumstances that might occur when you enter your boss' office for a conference. In the first situation the boss sits behind a large, imposing desk while you are invited to sit in a chair in front of the desk. In the second situation, however, the boss rises, invites you to be seated, and then sits in a chair next to you. The nonverbal messages are quite different. In the first, your subordinate status is reinforced; in the second it is significantly reduced. As a result, the nature of the discussion between you will probably be affected.

ARTIFACTS

By manipulating such things as hairstyles, dress, and visual aids, speakers can communicate nonverbally. As Knapp (1978) indicates, this fact is particularly true of clothing. "Sexual attraction, self-assertion, self-denial, concealment, group identification, display of status or role" are some of the nonverbal functions of clothing (p. 178). Cosmetics, jewelry, perfume, and wigs are additional examples of artifacts that send nonverbal messages.

Recently, two friends were invited to a dinner party. The hostess specifically requested that male guests wear coats and ties, and that female guests wear dresses or suits. One of the two friends indicated his intention to wear jeans, boots, and a Western-style shirt. He insisted that he would not allow someone to dictate what he should wear. Although socially questionable, this person definitely made a nonverbal statement which affected his interaction with the hostess and other guests at the party.

ENVIRONMENTAL FACTORS

The environment, or physical surroundings, can also be used as nonverbal communication. War protesters might assemble in a cemetery in order to emphasize the tragedy of war. A presidential candidate might begin a campaign at the site of a speech by Lincoln or Washington as a means of suggesting the potential greatness of the candidate. The way a person decorates his or her apartment or office may communicate that individual's tastes, interests, accomplishments, status, and so on. Someone entertaining a date might use dim lighting, a fire in the fireplace, or candlelight in order to create a romantic atmosphere.

THREE FACTS ABOUT NONVERBAL COMMUNICATION

It is important that, in addition to being aware of the various *types* of nonverbal messages, you also understand the *functions* of nonverbal messages. As a starting point, the following three facts can help you do a better job of understanding how the types of nonverbal behavior are used in human communication.

1. Most nonverbal communication occurs in groups, or clusters, rather than in isolation. When, for example, you encounter a friend in a theatre lobby, you might wave your hand, move your arm, and lean forward in order to attract his or her attention. You might also smile and move closer to the person in order to indicate that you are happy to see him or her. And your voice could indicate that you are interested in establishing or maintaining a relationship with the other person.

2. The second fact is that nonverbal communication is frequently used to establish the atmosphere or scene for communication. This means that humans use nonverbal messages in order to help others understand the nature of a particular situation. For example, if someone wants to share confidential information, he or she may move closer, speak in a soft voice, glance around the room to make sure that no one else is listening, and so on. Such behaviors assist the listener in understanding the nature of the communication that is to follow.

3. Some nonverbal behaviors, which Knapp (1978) refers to as "regulators," are used to "maintain and regulate the back and forth nature of speaking and listening between two or more interactants" (p. 16). Such behaviors include cues which indicate that a speaker wants to prevent another from speaking, or that someone is finished speaking. When, for example, a person leans back, folds his or her hands, and looks down, his or her cues indicate that he or she is finished speaking. Regulators are important, as they appear to be "on the periphery of our awareness and are generally difficult to inhibit." Furthermore, they are usually expressed nonverbally rather than verbally (Knapp, 1978, pp. 16–17).

PROBLEMS TO AVOID

The interpretation of nonverbal messages requires considerable caution. Knowing about nonverbal communication and interpreting it accurately are not the same thing. As Scheffler indicates in

Conditions of Knowledge, "a person might well have all the relevant information concerning some skill without having the skill itself . . . ." (1965, p. 92).

UNDERESTIMATING THE TASK

Most people are not as competent at interpreting nonverbal communication as they think. De Paulo and Rosenthal (1979) indicate, for example, that their study of nonverbal communication demonstrates that

> people's perceptions of their own decoding skills and of their attentional biases do not correspond at all to their actual skills and biases as measured by our instruments. (p. 242)

They conclude that people are generally incapable of making accurate assessments of their ability to use and to understand nonverbal factors in communication (1979, p. 239). As one who is striving to improve your listening effectiveness, you must not assume that interpreting speakers' nonverbal communication is a simple matter.

CONTEXTUAL PROBLEMS

Nonverbal communication should not be interpreted or understood apart from the context in which it occurs. Generally, meanings for specific nonverbal behaviors change from situation to situation and from one culture to another. In one situation placing your hand on another person's shoulder could communicate sympathy. In another situation, however, the same action could function to chastise someone for inappropriate, unacceptable behavior. Placing your feet on a desk at home might suggest that you are relaxed and comfortable, but the same behavior during an employment interview would probably be interpreted as disrespectful or as refusal to take the interview seriously.

If you notice that a person repeatedly glances at his or her watch during a conversation, you might conclude that the person is bored or disinterested. It could be, however, that he or she has an important meeting in a few minutes. This behavior could also mean that the person you're talking to is proud of a new watch and hopes that you will notice it. Thus in each situation the meaning for the same behavior differs significantly.

For one religious group, shouting, rolling on the floor, clapping hands, and so on are perfectly appropriate behaviors during a religious service. For another group, however, the same behaviors might be considered inappropriate and offensive. In some cultures arriving late to an appointment or social engagement is viewed as perfectly acceptable, polite behavior. But in another culture, being late is regarded as inconsiderate or rude.

The interpretation of nonverbal aspects of communication *can* have universal meanings, but even these must be understood in relation to the contexts in which they occur. Other aspects of nonverbal communication have no universal meanings. Still other forms of nonverbal communication can be understood only when you know the speaker very well and base your interpretations on such intimate knowledge (see Argyle, 1975, pp. 8, 59–61). Clearly, a little knowledge of nonverbal communication does not qualify anyone to make instant and flawless conclusions about a speaker or his or her message (Nierenberg and Calero, 1973, pp. 19–26).

Listening Lab

Improving the Nonverbal Dimension of Listening

* Don't underestimate the difficulty of interpreting nonverbal messages
* Consider context: nonverbal behaviors may have different meanings in different contexts
* Interpret verbal and nonverbal communication simultaneously
* Solicit feedback
* Avoid stereotyping by using the Recognition/Refusal/ Replacement system

STEREOTYPING

While the problem of stereotyping is closely related to contextual problems, it presents a particularly troublesome barrier to understanding nonverbal communication. Many people probably accept the idea that voice is a clear indicator of a person's personality and emotions. Thus, in spite of what a person says verbally, a truer index of feelings such as anger, fear, or anxiety can be ascertained by listening to the voice. A weak, quivering voice means that a speaker is nervous. Similarly, a strong, well-projected, forceful voice indicates that a speaker is competent, controlled, and self-assured. The problem of stereotyping throws such assumptions into serious question.

Stereotyping means that listeners have preconceived ideas about voice characteristics which they associate with certain personalities and feeling states. Unfortunately, such assumptions cannot be trusted. You can test this in several ways. You might listen to someone over the radio for a period of time and form a mental image of that person's appearance and personality. Later, when you see this person, you may be surprised to discover how far he or she misses the image you have constructed. You might assume that a deep, powerful voice is "masculine" only to discover that a person with such a voice contradicts your preconceived image. Similarly, if a woman's voice is deep, a careless listener might conclude that she will exhibit what he or she thinks are "masculine" characteristics, only to discover that she looks and acts much differently than expected. These kinds of problems led Starkweather (1961) to conclude that one must be "pessimistic concerning the usefulness of attempts to assess personality from nonverbal (vocal) stimuli" (p. 65). Likewise, Addington concluded, after reviewing the literature on voice and personality, that "whether we like it or not, our voices do elicit personality judgments which may or may not be consistent with more direct or valid personality assessments" (Addington, 1968, p. 493).

Stereotyping presents other problems for listeners. If you believe that nervous people behave in certain ways, frightened people exhibit specific characteristics, or that angry people always behave in certain ways, you probably respond more to stereotyped images than to what the speaker is actually doing or saying. You might be conversing with someone who speaks loudly, uses sweeping gestures, and pounds on a table. If you believe that these actions always mean that a person is angry, you may totally misunderstand. These behaviors may reflect a strong interest and involvement and desire for you to realize the importance of the point being made.

In another situation you might conclude that lack of eye contact, nervous mannerisms, and poor vocal projection indicate that a speaker is unsure of himself or herself and, consequently, dull and uninteresting. Actually, this speaker might feel intimidated or even frightened. He or she may habitually look down and away from a listener when attempting to think carefully. The verbal content may be interesting, but your attitude toward the person's nonverbal behavior could adversely affect your listening.

It is probably true, as authorities in nonverbal communication state, that people tend to pay more attention to nonverbal than to verbal communication; however, it does not follow that one's interpretations are necessarily correct when they are based upon stereotyped images of various nonverbal behaviors.

SUGGESTIONS FOR UNDERSTANDING NONVERBAL COMMUNICATION

Understanding nonverbal communication is no simple task. It requires knowledge, effort, and practice. If you understand the types of nonverbal messages that speakers send, the three facts about nonverbal communication, and the major problems to avoid when interpreting nonverbal messages, you should be in a good position to make significant progress in your ability to understand nonverbal communication. The following suggestions are intended to assist you in your efforts.

STUDY NONVERBAL COMMUNICATION

Make a conscious effort to observe the functioning of nonverbal communication in the classroom, at work, in meetings, at social functions, etc. As you do so, compare and contrast what you observe with the discussion in this chapter. Attempt to read about nonverbal communication in books and articles devoted to it. If possible, take a course in nonverbal communication. In short, learn as much as you can.

ALWAYS CONSIDER CONTEXTUAL FACTORS

In any listening situation you can significantly increase your ability to understand people's nonverbal communication if you consciously attempt to discover and to observe the contextual factors that influence and alter its meanings. Try to avoid assuming that nonverbal behaviors mean the same thing in every situation or for every group of people.

INTERPRET VERBAL AND NONVERBAL COMMUNICATION SIMULTANEOUSLY

As discussed in this chapter, verbal and nonverbal communication are interrelated. Nonverbal behavior may complement, contradict, reinforce, and regulate verbal messages. When contradictions occur, try to resolve them by carefully attending to the total verbal message and to clusters of nonverbal messages. The important thing to remember is that understanding verbal messages helps you to understand nonverbal messages and vice versa.

USE FEEDBACK TO CHECK YOUR PERCEPTIONS

Although nonverbal communication is sometimes unconscious (Argyle, 1975, p. 8), asking a speaker to explain his or her nonverbal behaviors may help your understanding. Also, requesting that someone respond to your interpretations of his or her nonverbal communication is a valuable way to check your understanding. In chapter 8 feedback is discussed as an important means of responding to speakers. You will be able to use ideas from that chapter as you attempt to follow this suggestion.

GUARD AGAINST STEREOTYPING

Make an effort to understand and recognize your stereotyped views of nonverbal communication. In any listening situation, try as hard as possible to understand people's nonverbal communication without letting your stereotypes interfere. Once again, you will probably need to apply *recognition, refusal,* and *replacement* in order to overcome this problem.

REFERENCES

Addington, D. W. "The Relationship of Selected Vocal Characteristics to Personality Perception." *Speech Monographs* 35 (1968), 492–503.

Argyle, M. *Bodily Communication.* New York: International Universities Press, 1975.

De Paulo, B. and R. Rosenthal. "Ambivalence, Discrepancy, and Deception in Nonverbal Communication." In *Skill in Nonverbal Communication: Individual Differences,* R. Rosenthal, ed. Cambridge, Mass.: Oelgeschlager, Gunn, and Hain, 1979, 204–248.

Harper, G., A. W. Wiens, and J. D. Matarazzo. *Nonverbal Communication: The State of the Art.* New York: John Wiley and Sons, 1978.

Knapp, M. L. *Nonverbal Communication in Human Interaction,* 2nd edition. New York: Holt, Rinehart and Winston, 1978.

Knapp, M. L. *Essentials of Nonverbal Communication,* New York: Holt, Rinehart and Winston, 1980.

Mehrabian, A. *Silent Messages: Implicit Communication of Emotions and Attitudes.* 2nd ed. Belmont, Calif.: Wadsworth, 1981.

Nierenberg, G. and H. Calero. *How to Read a Person Like a Book.* New York: Pocket Books, 1973.

Scheffler, I. *Conditions of Knowledge.* Glenview, Ill.: Scott, Foresman, 1965.

Starkweather, J. A. "Vocal Communication of Personality and Human Feeling." *Journal of Communication* 11 (1961), 63–72.

Wood, J. T. *Human Communication: A Symbolic Interactionist Perspective.* New York: Holt, Rinehart and Winston, 1982.

KEY TERMS

Nonverbal communication

Kinesics

Physical characteristics

Touching

Paralanguage

Proxemics

Artifacts

Environmental factors

Underestimating the task

Context

Stereotyping

EXERCISES

1. Divide into small groups. Assign each person a particular attitude to assume throughout the discussion; ask them to convey the attitude *nonverbally.* At the end of the discussion each person in the group should attempt to decide which person was assigned what attitude. Discuss the accuracy of the predictions.

2. Attend a movie of your choice. As you watch the movie, attempt to determine specific uses of nonverbal communication as a means of establishing the characters.

3. In a restaurant, student union, airport, bus depot, etc., you and a partner from class should observe the nonverbal behaviors of specified people whom you both agree to observe. Later, discuss similarities and differences in your observations and conclusions.

4. Ask a friend to allow you to describe his or her characteristic nonverbal behaviors. Then ask your friend to respond to the accuracy of your observations. Explain ways in which you were correct and/or mistaken in your perceptions.

5. Engage in a conversation with someone you know well. During the conversation, attempt to minimize your use of nonverbal communication. Then ask the other person to respond to your participation in the discussion.

C H A P T E R

6

UNDERSTANDING VERBAL MESSAGES

OBJECTIVES

1. *To appreciate the importance of understanding the speaker's verbal messages.*
2. *To understand how experience, context, biases, and fear of failure affect your ability to understand speakers.*
3. *To begin the process of improving your vocabulary as a means of improving your listening ability.*
4. *To initiate notetaking practices that eliminate interferences and enhance understanding.*

Effective listening requires more than hearing and attending to messages. As necessary and important as these skills are, you must also strive to understand what you hear and attend to. Although you are probably capable of accurate comprehension most of the time, there are occasions in which you may discover that you are unfamiliar with a speaker's words and/or ideas. There are also times in which your meaning for a speaker's words may differ significantly from the speaker's meanings. Such situations can lead to misunderstanding and, consequently, ineffective listening and communication.

Certainly the speaker plays an important role in helping listeners understand his or her message. Effective speakers realize this and make every effort to analyze their listeners carefully enough to present messages which will probably be meaningful to them. If a speaker fails to do this successfully, you may complain that he or she is "talking over your head" or trying to overwhelm you with "big words" that you can't understand.

Actually, communication works best when *both* speaker and listener strive to cooperate for the purpose of creating shared meaning. But since this is a book about listening improvement you should focus your attention on ways in which you can maximize your ability to understand speakers—even when they fall short of upholding their end of the communication process.

MEANING

Comprehension is closely related to the concept of meaning. One perspective for studying meaning is symbolic interactionism. As Wood (1982) suggests, symbolic interactionism is based upon three principles:

(1) Human beings act toward phenomena on the basis of the meanings they attach to the phenomena. (2) These meanings arise in social

contexts. (3) Through an interpretative process of self-communication the individual modifies and manages particular meanings. (p. 69)

The first principle suggests that meaning does not reside in things or in behavior. Instead, human beings attach meaning to various phenomena. Things exist but have no meaning until people give them meaning. And as Wood (1982) says, "the meanings that individuals attach to external phenomena" are what "guide behavior" (p. 67).

The second principle implies that the meanings which people attach to things are not totally individual. Instead, meanings result from interaction with others. Thus, the ways in which you attach meaning to anything are largely influenced by your experiences with other people. This fact helps explain why meanings are shared (Wood, 1982, p. 68).

Finally, Wood indicates that meaning is not totally a matter of taking on others' meanings as your own. You must relate something to your situation at a given time, your feelings, and your past experiences in order to interpret its meaning for you. Meanings are partially shared and partially a matter of individual interpretation (Wood, 1982, pp. 68–69). Your meanings belong to you, but at the same time you should attempt, as an effective listener, to understand the speaker's meanings.

Barriers to understanding may occur when you lack necessary or appropriate experience, when you are unable to use the context to interpret the meaning of another's symbols, and when your emotional responses affect your ability to interpret another's symbols (see Barker, 1981, pp. 78–83). Whenever your meaning differs significantly from the speaker's meaning, misunderstanding can occur. The following discussion attempts to assist you to minimize such problems.

EXPERIENCE

Recently I tested one of my listening classes over material which was presented orally. Some of the students later complained that the test was unfair. They explained that some people in the class were more familiar with the material than others. Their past experiences with the material, it was argued, made it easier for them to do well on the test than for those who had no past experiences with the material presented.

While these arguments were correct, the persons making them had missed an important point about listening effectiveness. In any listening situation, the person whose experiences provide knowledge and understanding of the subject discussed can enjoy an advantage over the one who has no idea what the speaker is talking about. Experience with the speaker's topic makes it easier to interpret the speaker's meaning.

Not long ago I attended a series of lecture/discussions on Jewish-Christian dialogue. One of the speakers, a professor of Judaic studies, spoke on the theological dilemma of the holocaust. Specifically, he spoke on the writings of Elie Wiesel, a holocaust survivor. Since I knew relatively little about Jewish views of the holocaust and still less about the works of Wiesel, I did some reading prior to the lecture, particularly from some of Wiesel's works. Such reading proved to be quite helpful when I later attended the lecture. Additionally, the reading, the lecture, and the discussions which followed proved to be of value to me when listening to later discussions and news reports regarding events in the Middle East.

Experience can be direct or indirect, but the more you are willing to increase and vary your experiences the more you enable yourself to understand other people. The well-read person, the person who works in a variety of jobs, the person who travels extensively, and the person who participates in a wide variety of activities will have less difficulty understanding new subjects and new material.

CONTEXT

When a speaker's words and phrases are unfamiliar, the context provides you with a means of understanding messages. If, for example, a friend uses a word that has no clear meaning for you, your experiences with the surrounding words may prove helpful. You may not recognize a word like *infatuation,* but the context in which it is used may help you to attach a meaning similar to that of the speaker. The context may make it clear that it involves the strong emotional attachment which one person has for another: "All he can do is think about Ann. He can't eat or sleep. I guess it's a bad case of infatuation."

Knowing the context of a word or message is also helpful because the meanings which people assign to words often vary from one context to another. A word such as *love* must almost always be understood in context. A person may say, "I love my dog" in one situation and "I love my spouse" in another. Shooting an eagle may be a serious violation of the law in one situation but an outstanding accomplishment in golf. Longtime friends may call each other "old fools" as an expression of affection, but calling someone an old fool in another context would be taken much differently.

BIASES

Imagine a person is attending a meeting in which crime is the topic of discussion. Assume that this individual has strong feelings about crime and the treatment of criminals, believing that our society is soft on crime and criminals. One speaker at this meeting is a probation-parole officer. The chairperson announces that the speaker's talk is entitled "The Need for Probation and Parole in the Criminal Justice System." The listener's immediate response is negative, as he or she thinks, "Another bleeding heart who wants to turn criminals loose to commit more crimes." But let us assume that, instead of giving in to an impulse to turn the speaker off, to refuse to understand, or to argue silently with the speaker while waiting for an opportunity to attack during the question-and-answer period, this listener decides to attend to the speech, concluding that "even though I have my doubts, I'll see what the speaker has to offer." Such a decision is an important first step—a willingness to try to understand the speaker.

As the speaker indicates that large numbers of people are being given probation and parole as an alternative to prison, the listener may react emotionally, thinking that he or she was right. The speaker is another "liberal" who is "soft on crime." But again, the listener manages to force such thoughts to the background and attempts to listen to the speaker's explanation: Statistics indicate that it costs far less to supervise people on parole or probation than to house, feed, and clothe them in prison. Furthermore, if all of those people on probation were imprisoned, more prisons would have to be built. Also, when people are in prison, taxpayers often must pay welfare for their dependents. Having a job while on probation or parole reduces this problem.

At this point the listener admits that the speaker has some good points. On the other hand, he or she may think, "That's all well and good, but it still doesn't address the problem of letting criminals out on the streets." Before deciding that the speaker has avoided the "real" issue, however, the listener continues to pay attention as the speaker explains that most parole and probation violators are not serious offenders, such as murderers (who actually have the lowest return rate), but are minor offenders, such as bad check passers. Had the listener tuned the speaker out, he or she might have missed this argument.

This illustration is intended to emphasize the importance of the relationship between understanding and the ability to set biases aside. All that you are asked to do is to make an effort to keep your biases from getting in the way of understanding. It does not mean that you should abandon your beliefs and feelings; rather it means that you should try to understand others *prior* to making evaluations and judgments. It is not easy, particularly when your experiences and beliefs have led you to hold strong feelings. Once again, the process of changing behavior requires a continuous effort to practice the three steps of recognition, refusal, and replacement.

THE FEAR OF FAILURE

A major problem with fear of failure is that it seldom emerges as a clearly expressed reason for ineffective listening. Instead, it is frequently disguised as another reason. For example, a listener who is afraid of failing to grasp difficult material may declare the subject or speaker dull and uninteresting. People for whom a refusal to listen is the result of a fear of failing are more comfortable rationalizing or finding a scapegoat.

Fear of failure is one of our two most common fears. The other is fear of rejection, and it relates closely to the fear of failure in that "people are often afraid to fail for the very reason that they might be rejected if they do" (Hauck, 1975, p. 16). Because the fear of failure is significant, "the individual motivated by a fear of failure is going to select the strategy that gets him away from the failure experience" (Birney, Burdick, and Teevan, 1969, p. 12). In relation to listening and understanding, this fact suggests that the fear of failure can actually prevent listeners from making an effort to understand, especially in difficult listening situations.

One way to avoid failure is to refuse to try. Essentially this means giving up, admitting defeat, and dismissing yourself from the listening situation. A second way to avoid failure is to belittle the listening situation and content as trivial, unimportant, or silly. Such occasions can be treated "as games" or something to be treated "lightheartedly." A third method is to lower your goals and expectations sufficiently to avoid the risk of failing. Thus, if you cannot comprehend significant portions of a message you simply conclude that you got all you wanted or needed; the parts you did not understand are declared unimportant or irrelevant. Fourth, you can seek out listening situations "that are easy—that is, without much conflict or challenge." You thus assure yourself that you will not have to come to grips with failing to understand a speaker and his or her message (Wood, 1976, pp. 81–82).

The first step in approaching difficult material is to realize that everyone fails at times and that there is nothing "bad" or disgraceful about failing. Highly accomplished people often experience numerous failures on the way to success. A young scholar, who is today one of the leading authorities in classical rhetoric, began writing for publication as a graduate student. He sent out manuscript after manuscript only to receive rejections for all of them. Instead of viewing the rejections as proof of his inability, this young man studied each rejection and referees' comments with great care. He learned to profit from his failures and is today a respected and widely published scholar.

A second step is to realize that failure to understand can actually be a form of understanding. Discovering what you do not know and understand tells you what you need to do to improve your understanding. For example, a young woman sat in on a number of conversations among a group of avid chess players. She did not know much about the game and felt frustrated and ignorant listening to her friends' use of terminology associated with chess. This experience led her to read some books on chess and to seek the help of a friend who knew the game and was willing to spend some time teaching her how to play. In this way the young woman turned feelings of failure into the development of a new interest.

As already suggested, listening improvement is a personal matter. There is no proof or absolute guarantee that overcoming the fear of failure will turn you instantly into an effective listener. But learning to overcome fear of failure is an important step, one which can help you increase your ability to understand even when the material you listen to is difficult.

VOCABULARY EXPANSION

An inadequate vocabulary is frequently a reason for misunderstanding. It can lead to at least two specific problems: (1) The listener may be unable to attach meanings to a speaker's words, and (2) The meanings which a listener attaches may differ significantly from the speaker's meanings for the words. It follows, therefore, that vocabulary expansion is a valuable means of increasing your capacity to listen effectively (Wolff, Marsnik, Tacey, and Nichols, 1983, p. 80).

This discussion of vocabulary expansion is not intended to

Listening Lab

Improving the Verbal Dimension of Listening

* Increase your verbal experience and expertise
* Study and consider verbal context to interpret meaning
* Set aside biases and emotions
* Overcome the fear of failure:
    Don't refuse to try.
    Don't belittle the situation.
    Don't lower your goals.
    Don't look for easy listening situations.

suggest that increasing your vocabulary will solve all of your listening problems. It will not, for example, guarantee that you will understand a speaker's ideas, concepts, and feelings. On the other hand, it is important to keep in mind that "without an understanding of words, comprehension is impossible" (Rubin, 1983, p. 66). Thus, increasing your vocabulary constitutes one means of assuring that you can do a more effective job of understanding other people.

READING

One way to increase your vocabulary is to read as much and as widely as possible. As Dale, O'Rourke, and Bamman (1971) indicate, "Reading is probably the single greatest contributing factor to the building of an extensive vocabulary" (p. 244).

The major advantage of increasing your vocabulary through reading is that you can use the context in which the words occur as a means of helping to figure out the meanings of unfamiliar words. You can then add them to your vocabulary. For example, assume that you are reading a story and come across an unfamiliar word. As previously discussed, the way that the word is used in a sentence, or throughout the story, can help you to learn the meaning of the word as intended by the author. You can do this by comparing and contrasting it with familiar words in the context. If, for example, a writer were to say, "the parsimonious old man could not accept his daughter's unselfish tendency to share her money with people in need," the context suggests that "parsimonious" is the opposite of *unselfish, giving, generous.* Thus, you should be able to figure out that "parsimonious" means stingy, selfish, frugal.

WORD STUDY

In conjunction with reading, and often as a result of it, you can increase your vocabulary by developing an interest in words. Studying the following types of words is beneficial: synonyms (words with similar meanings); antonyms (words with opposite meanings); homographs (words which are spelled the same but have different meanings); and homonyms (words pronounced the same but with different meanings). Studying word origins (etymology), prefixes, suffixes, and roots; figures of speech; and word games are additional means of strengthening your vocabulary (Dale, O'Rourke, and Bamman, 1971, p. 15). Dictionaries are also a valuable word study tool. You should keep in mind, however, that "dictionaries do not prescribe or make rules about word meanings and pronunciations"; they describe current uses and meanings (Rubin, 1983, p. 92). Looking up unfamiliar words from your reading or listening can certainly serve as a starting point for learning new words.

VARIED EXPERIENCES

Since the purpose of increasing your vocabulary is to improve your ability to understand speakers, it makes sense to observe and to study words as people use them—in a wide variety of settings, events, and situations. Experiences such as travel, jobs, memberships and participation in organizations, and hobbies are examples of opportunities which can help you expand your vocabulary. Movies, plays, conversations with interesting people, periodicals, and selected television viewing offer additional opportunities. It is also advisable to seek opportunities to speak and write. Such activities make it necessary for you to pay attention to words and meanings.

A SYSTEMATIC APPROACH

As discussed in chapter 3, the establishment of desirable habits requires conscious effort and practice. It may prove helpful, therefore, to approach vocabulary building systematically. The following suggestions, based partially upon Rubin (1983, pp. 78–79), provide an approach to increasing your awareness and understanding of words and their various meanings:

1. Be alert for words which you do not know, or which are used in unusual or unfamiliar ways.

2. In reading or listening, try to use the context to figure out meanings of words.

3. Provide feedback to speakers as a means of seeking clarification regarding their meanings.

4. Write down unfamiliar words from your reading and listening and look them up later.

5. Keep a notebook in which you record new words and their various meanings.

6. Pay attention to connotative meanings, the meanings which people attach to words through experience and feeling. This will help you to understand words beyond their dictionary meanings.

7. If possible, take courses in the history of the English language, semantics, general semantics, linguistics, composition, creative writing, and so on.

8. Attempt to maintain an active interest in language and vocabulary.

A PERSPECTIVE FOR VOCABULARY IMPROVEMENT

On one hand, the importance and relevance of vocabulary to listening comprehension cannot be reasonably denied. As indicated earlier in this chapter, if you are unable to attach appropriate meanings to a speaker's words—if you have no idea what he or she is talking about—it is extremely difficult to imagine that you can understand the message. In this sense, vocabulary improvement is an essential aspect of listening comprehension.

On the other hand, vocabulary improvement does not in itself lead to listening comprehension. It is one important means of improving your ability to understand speakers and their ideas. Thus, vocabulary improvement must not be used in isolation. A knowledge of dictionary meanings or a good reading vocabulary does not automatically lead to successful understanding in a variety of listening situations. Instead, vocabulary improvement must be combined with the acquisition of varied experiences, general learning, and an understanding of communication and communication contexts. You should also strive to prevent your biases from affecting your interpretation of speakers' messages, and you must avoid allowing fear of failure to keep you from working to improve your ability to understand others and their ideas.

NOTETAKING

Notetaking is a universal practice among students listening to lectures in school, but it is also used in business meetings, interviews, conferences, and so on. Potentially, notetaking has the advantage of encouraging active involvement in the listening process. It is also a valuable means of recording information and concepts for later review and additional study. As such, it can provide listeners with a means of remembering and understanding on a long-term basis.

There is a variety of commonly used notetaking procedures. One method is to construct an outline of the speaker's presentation. This procedure is of little value if the speaker is disorganized (see Wolff, Marsnik, et al., 1983, p. 90). Another method is to write summary statements of key information and explanations. A third method is to divide your notes into two columns. In one column you record key facts; then, in the corresponding position in the second column, you record details and explanations. It is also possible to combine these notetaking methods and tailor them to your own needs as a listener.

During more than twenty years of teaching—in high school, adult education, training sessions, and two universities—I have observed that successful students use a variety of notetaking techniques. For that reason I do not intend to prescribe which type of notetaking you should use. Instead, I am concerned with ways in which notetaking can thwart understanding and, in effect, prove counterproductive to effective listening.

NOTETAKING AND INATTENTION

As previously noted, attention is a prerequisite for understanding. It is extremely difficult to understand someone's message if your attention is elsewhere. Yet listeners can get so involved in taking notes, especially in trying to write down the speaker's exact words, that they lose the well-known advantage thought speed has over speaking speed (Nichols, 1969). As a result, you can get so bogged down trying to record information in your notes that you fail to pay attention to subsequent portions of the message. In this way notetaking can actually interfere with understanding.

You can prevent this interference by taking notes in your own words, developing abbreviations, and organizing and rewriting notes later. Also, as Wolvin and Coakley suggest (1982, p. 95), you should consider *not* taking notes, particularly when you will use the information immediately, when you can remember the information just as well without taking notes, and when concentrating on the presentation is more useful than taking notes.

NOTETAKING AND FACTS

Our society appears to place considerable emphasis and value on facts. Such commonly used expressions as "the facts speak for themselves," "just give us the facts," and "you can't argue with the facts" attest to this emphasis. Additionally—and perhaps as a result of stressing the importance of facts—testing in our educational system has frequently placed a premium on remembering and reciting factual material. As a practical matter, therefore, people often feel that notetaking should focus upon facts.

As important as facts are, they mean very little in and of themselves. They must be explained, interpreted, and applied to something. They are also used to support assertions and to establish conclusions. In notetaking it is important for you to take notes on explanations, concepts, ideas, and opinions as well as on the facts used to establish and support ideas and positions. When your notetaking ignores these matters you limit your ability to understand. Reviewing facts without understanding how they are used or what they explain is of very limited value.

Even when you are in situations which require you to record and memorize factual material, there is no law which states that you must restrict your listening to facts. Remember that you can still attempt to take notes which will help you to understand the material presented.

SUGGESTIONS FOR NOTETAKING

1. Decide whether you really need to take notes.

2. Never think of notetaking as a substitute for attention and understanding; it merely supplements and aids these processes.

3. Review and clarify your notes soon after taking them.

4. Indicate material which is especially important and/or which you need to study more extensively. This can be done through underlining, marginal notes, and so on.

5. Take notes on explanations and concepts as well as facts.

A PERSPECTIVE FOR NOTETAKING

As with vocabulary improvement, notetaking will not automatically improve your understanding of messages. You can very well take copious notes and have little or no idea what the speaker meant. This is precisely the reason for stating that notetaking is not a substitute for listening.

If you avoid limiting your notetaking to lists of facts, however, there are a variety of ways in which you can enhance your understanding. First, taking notes helps you to focus and maintain attention on the speaker, allowing you to use your mental free time more efficiently. Second, close attention aids you in placing material into your long-term memory. While memory is not the same as comprehension, remembering one thing can help you to understand subsequent material. Third, notetaking, especially if it focuses on explanations, can assist you in reviewing and studying the material. Combined with such behaviors as the use of feedback, additional reading, and varying your experiences, studying your notes can definitely help you in your efforts to understand what you hear.

In summary, notetaking can help you to get involved in listening, to review information, and to remember what you have heard. It is not, however, a substitute for listening. If carelessly or inappropriately used, notetaking can interfere with attention and can actually get in the way of understanding what you hear.

REFERENCES

Barker, L. L. *Communication.* 2nd ed. Englewood Cliffs, N.J.: Prentice-Hall, 1981.

Birney, R. C., H. Burdick, and R. C. Teevan. *Fear of Failure.* New York: Van Nostrand-Reinhold, 1969.

Dale, E., J. O'Rourke, and H. Bamman. *Techniques of Teaching Vocabulary.* Palo Alto, Calif.: Field Education Publications, 1971.

Hauck, P. A. *Overcoming Worry and Fear.* Philadelphia: Westminster Press, 1975.

Nichols, R. G. "Listening Is a 10-Part Skill." In *Readings in Interpersonal and Organizational Communication,* R. C. Huseman *et al.,* eds. Boston: Holbrook Press, 1969, 472–479.

Rubin, D. *Teaching Reading and Study Skills in Content Areas.* New York: Holt, Rinehart and Winston, 1983.

Wolff, F. I., N. C. Marsnik, W. S. Tacey, and R. G. Nichols. *Perceptive Listening.* New York: Holt, Rinehart and Winston, 1983.

Wolvin, A. D. and C. G. Coakley. *Listening.* Dubuque, Iowa: Wm. C. Brown, 1982.

Wood, J. T. *What Are You Afraid Of?* Englewood Cliffs, N.J.: Prentice-Hall, 1976.

Wood, J. T. *Human Communication: A Symbolic Interactionist Perspective.* New York: Holt, Rinehart and Winston, 1982.

KEY TERMS

Meaning

Understanding

Symbolic interaction

Context

Experience

Bias

Fear of failure

Vocabulary

Notetaking

EXERCISES

1. As someone reads or plays a recording of material containing difficult vocabulary, make note of words which you do not understand. Then, try to determine the extent to which difficult words interfered with your ability to understand the message. It might be beneficial to reread or replay some or all of the message in conjunction with the class discussion.

2. Once a day for one week, read in a book, magazine, or scholarly journal that you find difficult to understand. Each time that you find an unfamiliar word look up a definition that seems to fit the context in which you encountered the word. Write the word and its definition in a notebook. Each time you hear or read any of the words on your list make a mark next to that word.

3. Listen to a speaker who takes a position with which you strongly disagree. Keep track of the number of times you catch yourself feeling angry, wanting to argue with the speaker, or wanting to "tune out" and think about something else. Compare notes and discuss your experience with other people.

4. When taking notes in your classes make a concentrated effort to take notes on your instructors' *explanations* rather than merely writing down facts, lists, etc. Try to do this for all lectures prior to an examination. Analyze the results.

5. In a conversation with a friend make an effort to supply feedback, but avoid initiating new topics, making judgmental statements, or arguing with your friend. Analyze the quality of the conversation, noting how you felt about it, any reactions (verbal or nonverbal) from your friend, and the relative amount of time each of you spent as a speaker or a listener.

6. As you listen to daily lectures or presentations, keep a list of words and phrases that are unfamiliar or difficult. Look them up and include their definitions in your notes. Over a period of time, assess the extent to which this procedure helped you to understand the material presented.

7. Choose several listening situations which you consider difficult and challenging. Make an effort to take fewer notes and concentrate on listening to the speakers. Observe the results and discuss your experience with others.

CHAPTER

7

ANALYZING AND EVALUATING MESSAGES

OBJECTIVES

1. *To understand the role and importance of analysis and evaluation in the listening process.*
2. *To understand why you should practice suspension of judgment in listening.*
3. *To begin applying criteria for evaluating support material and reasoning in a variety of listening situations.*
4. *To be able to distinguish between factual and nonfactual support material.*
5. *To understand how to analyze and evaluate propaganda.*

I n Goss' model of the listening process (see chapter 1), the evaluation of messages occurs primarily at the level of reflective processing. Although you may think of evaluation as applicable only to critical listening, it is not necessarily restricted to any one type of listening. In appreciative listening, for example, you might evaluate the material and the performance quality of a reader's theatre production or a dramatic interpretation of a play. And in various interpersonal situations you might evaluate the ideas, opinions, or advice of a friend.

You should realize, however, that evaluating is more than merely expressing an opinion or judgment. As a listening skill, it involves making careful assessments based upon a thorough understanding of a message. The purpose of this chapter is to assist you in improving your ability to analyze and evaluate messages intelligently and fairly.

ANALYSIS AND EVALUATION

Analysis refers to the act of examining a message, its content, purpose, support, audience, and social context (see Campbell, 1972, pp. 14–21). The analysis of a message might be accomplished informally, as in the case of interpersonal or appreciative listening, or it may be more formal and systematic, as in speech criticism. By examining the constituent parts of a message, analysis paves the way for evaluation.

Essentially, evaluation is the *rendering of a judgment on a message which you have heard, attended to, and understood.* It might consist of little more than saying, "I didn't like what she said." Or, it might consist of an extensive, formal judgment, based upon a specific set of evaluative standards. Thus, when you evaluate a message you attempt to make an assessment of its worth or value to you and/or to others. As Cathcart (1981) indicates, "students bent on improving written and oral discourse [skills] need not become rhetorical scholars or professional critics" (p. 14). They do, however, need to be reasonably knowledgeable in the areas of speech and criticism (p. 14).

THE SUSPENSION OF JUDGMENT

A first step in effective evaluation is to understand and practice the suspension of judgment. Evaluating a message *prior* to understanding and analyzing it constitutes a serious listening problem. Problems such as listening with biases, the entertainment syndrome, and fear of difficult material are frequently involved in premature evaluation.

Premature evaluation can occur in interpersonal situations, group discussions, public speaking settings, and mass communication presentations. On the interpersonal level, consider the true example of a man who told of ending a friendship with a person he had known for several years because his friend made a statement critical of his religion. In a group discussion someone decided that one member of the group was "a worthless troublemaker" because that person disagreed with one of his or her ideas. A university professor, when asked if he was going to attend a public speech by a controversial figure said, "No. She has nothing to say worth listening to." And when a college class was asked whether they listened to the President's State of the Union Address they gave responses such as "Why listen? He never says anything," and "Politics is boring." In each one of those examples someone is judging prior to hearing the speaker out, prior to making an attempt to understand the speaker.

Even after hearing and understanding a speaker you are not obligated to make an instant judgment. Evaluation can and sometimes should be a long-term process. An effective listener might suspend judgment more or less indefinitely. As one reads, gains new experiences, listens to additional messages from the same or from other speakers he or she can eventually arrive to the point of making a judgment. For example, you might have a conversation or discussion with someone, listen carefully, make every effort to understand the person, and engage in preliminary analysis and evaluation. You may, however, engage in additional conversations, observe him or her in a variety of situations, add to your own experiences, and possibly learn more about interpersonal communication. These factors could either strengthen or alter your earlier judgments.

ANALYZING AND EVALUATING SUPPORT MATERIAL

In order to evaluate a speaker's ideas, arguments, and reasons it is often necessary to examine and evaluate the support which the speaker uses to back up his or her positions. This aspect of listening appears to relate more to discriminative, comprehensive, and critical listening than to listening for appreciation (enjoyment) or interpersonal listening.

EVALUATING FACTUAL SUPPORT

As Ehninger (1974) indicates, "facts are not easy to define." Generally, however, facts are "those things men believe to be the case, either because they have experienced them first hand or because they are regarded as the truthfully reported experiences of others" (pp. 51–52). Facts can be presented in a variety of forms. They can consist of reports of *direct observation of various phenomena.* They can be *statistics* or *specific examples.* And they can consist of a type of demonstration in which *the actual object is presented as evidence.* In courts of law the latter kind of evidence is referred to as *real* evidence. The following methods of testing these types of evidence are based on Ehninger (1974, pp. 55–60) and Eisenberg and Ilardo (1980, pp. 43–50).

In evaluating the *statistical* presentation of facts you should consider a variety of criteria. The first concerns the statistician's methodology. If a study indicated that the reported results of an experiment were equally the result of chance and experimental treatment, there would be little reason to accept the finding. This is so even when the reporting is carefully worded: "This finding shows a possible trend . . . ."

The sample from which the statistics are derived is also quite important. If an interviewer seeks out twenty high school students who have been in trouble with legal and/or school authorities because of drug abuse and then concludes that "90 percent of all local high school students surveyed admit to taking illegal drugs," the sample leads to extremely misleading conclusions. The listener needs to know whether the survey included every individual in a population; whether the survey was based on a random sample, meaning that each individual in the population had an equal chance of being observed; or whether it was a survey based on a stratified sample in which a small portion of a population is selected in proportion to the characteristics of the entire population.

Also, it is important to consider the objectivity, ability, motivation, and accuracy of both the person who compiles the statistics *and* the person who presents or reports them. Statistics must be compiled and reported by objective observers, not by those who have reason to want the results to support their interests or biases. You should be cautious, for example, if you hear a scientist for the Tobacco Institute report statistics to support the assertion that smoking is harmless.

When listening to speakers who use *factual examples,* consider two points. First, is the sample from which the example is drawn too small to justify a conclusion about the entire population? If one speaker has examined only twenty of a population of two hundred people, while another speaker has studied one hundred fifty, the larger number of examples would be preferable. Similarly, an example that is exceptional should not be reported as representing the whole. If two employees in an organization consistently take paid sick days when they are not actually ill, it does not mean that such behavior is typical of all the employees in that organization. While the two exceptional cases may indeed be factual, they do not represent the behavior of all employees.

If a speaker presents *real objects* as evidence, you should ask, first, whether the object actually is what it is reported to be. It is possible to present imitations or forgeries as the real item. If someone wants to convince you that UFOs are real he or she might present photographs purporting to prove the existence of such "space craft." Yet photographs can be altered or "faked." Similarly, someone could alter a worthless object to make it appear as an authentic antique. Second, it is important for you to know whether an actual object, like an example, is representative. A house painter might show you his or her one successful job while not showing you a dozen unsatisfactory jobs. The one you see is well painted but not necessarily representative of the painter's work. Facts are not inherently or automatically good evidence.

EVALUATING NONFACTUAL SUPPORT

Nonfactual support is frequently used to clarify, add interest, or reinforce factual support. It is not necessarily less valuable than factual support, but it does call for different standards of evaluation. A person who might not accept or understand factual support may respond positively to nonfactual support. A child might be unmoved by all kinds of facts regarding the telling of lies, but the story of "The Boy Who Cried Wolf" might help him/her to understand that lying is wrong.

When a speaker uses nonfactual support to illustrate a point, he or she might present stories, hypothetical examples, quotations from literature, figurative analogies, and so on. As a listener you should be careful to distinguish between nonfactual and factual support, and you should realize that nonfactual support is used for different purposes than factual support. As Freeley (1981) suggests, factual support is used "to establish a high degree of probability" or "logical proof." Nonfactual support falls under what Freeley refers to as "ethical or emotional proof," meaning that it is useful for "illustrating a point, and in making a vivid impression on the audience" (p. 119).

Another approach to the evaluation of nonfactual support is provided by Larson's (1973) discussion of "unifying" and "pragmatic" styles: The unifying speaker's audience is essentially receptive and supportive of the speaker's position. Such a speaker is not trying to change minds as much as he or she is attempting "to whip up their enthusiasm or to give them encouragement and dedication." Pragmatic speakers, in contrast, "must win an audience" and "cannot afford to take the risk of appealing to abstract ideals" (p. 64). Thus the unifying speaker can more appropriately rely on nonfactual, figurative, illustrative support (pp. 64–66).

EVALUATING A SPEAKER'S REASONING

Support material and reasoning are not functionally separate; that is, speakers reason with support material in an attempt to establish their conclusions. According to Ziegelmueller and Dause, "an argument consists of three basic elements." These are "the data, the reasoning process, and the conclusion." The "reasoning process is the procedure which associates data in order to give it meaning" (Ziegelmueller and Dause, 1975, pp. 85–86). Their definitions indicate data (factual and expert support) must be used in order to support a conclusion.

CAUSAL REASONING

When a speaker reasons causally, he or she reasons that the existence or presence of one thing or situation produces (causes) another thing or situation. This reasoning may also begin with the effect and argue that it was produced by a certain cause.

Suppose a speaker makes the following statement: "We can see that high school and elementary teachers are doing a poor job of teaching when we observe the rapid decline of scores on achievement tests and college entrance exams." The speaker is reasoning from cause to effect, maintaining that low test scores are caused by poor teaching. This statement also implies another use of causal reasoning, suggesting that scores on examinations are the result of teacher effectiveness or competence.

On the other hand, a speaker might argue from effect to cause. A politician might argue that existing economic problems like high inflation and interest rates are the result (effect) of careless spending on the part of a previous administration (cause). The assumption is that careless spending causes inflation and high interest rates. Support would consist of quoting of facts relevant to inflation and interest rates.

The listener who attempts to evaluate causal reasoning should use at least four criteria: (1) Is the asserted cause capable of producing the effect? (2) Are other causes ignored or omitted? (3) Is the speaker mistaking coincidence for causality? (4) Is the speaker confusing a time sequence for causality?

The first criterion considers whether the asserted cause is strongly and sufficiently linked to the effect. Imagine a situation in which a person seeks a position as a personnel director. The employing official asks the applicant whether he or she is qualified for the position. The applicant replies that he or she took three college courses in personnel. The employer would be wise to require additional evidence.

The second criterion considers the issue of multiple causality. More often than not, a variety of causes produces an effect. If someone says that crime in the United States is caused by violence on television, he or she is probably guilty of ignoring multiple causes. As a means of testing this assertion, you might ask whether crime would disappear were all television sets abolished.

The third criterion cautions you to be aware of situations in which coincidence is confused with causality. Correlation, or a time and space relationship, does not automatically establish causality. Consider a speech in which someone suggests that food in the employee's cafeteria is unfit to eat because there were 200 cases of indigestion reported, and in every case the worker ate in the cafeteria. This fact alone fails to establish causality, for there is no reason to believe that 200 cases of indigestion would not occur regardless of where the people happen to eat.

Listening Lab

Improving the Analytical/Evaluative Dimension of Listening

* Distinguish between factual and nonfactual support material
* Apply the tests for factual support
* Evaluate the appropriateness of speakers' use of nonfactual support
* Understand the relationship between support and reasoning
* Apply the tests for reasoning
* Monitor ethical and unethical uses of propaganda

Finally, you should be aware that the occurrence of events in a certain time sequence does not automatically establish causality. Simply because one thing happens and another follows, you cannot assume that the first thing caused the second. You should be suspicious, for example, if you hear someone say, "All the financial problems which our state is suffering resulted from electing Smith. It's time to elect a governor who will not lead us down the path of financial ruin." Clearly, it is questionable to assume that financial problems that followed Smith's election were automatically caused by Smith. You should require a stronger link.

ANALOGY

Reasoning by analogy is based on the following assumption: for items, people, or situations that are alike in most essential respects, what is true of one will be true of the other. A student using this kind of reasoning might say, "Carol and I have always received the same grade in classes which we have both taken. If she got an A in The History of Philosophy, so will I." Such reasoning depends primarily on the likeness of the things being compared. If there are important differences, the comparison will be invalid. If Carol and her friend have the same instructor and similar course content, the comparison might hold true. But if Carol's friend has a more demanding instructor who hardly ever gives A's, the comparison will be thrown into serious question.

REASONING BY EXAMPLE

Reasoning by example is reasoning in which one or several instances are presented as representative of a larger population of such instances. A friend tells you about three people who successfully supplemented their income by selling a certain product part-time, and suggests that you can do the same. The implication is that these three people are typical of all people who sell the product as a part-time endeavor. But if these people are exceptional—if *most* people who have tried to sell the product have failed—then the examples do not reasonably support the speaker's point. Reasoning by example is unreasonable unless the examples are *typical* (see Ziegelmueller and Dause on "typicality," 1975, pp. 113–114).

Closely related to typicality is the consideration of numbers of examples. This means that you should ask whether *enough* instances were examined to justify the speaker's conclusion. A researcher interested in learning about a species of animal might study a number of animals belonging to that species. In the course of the examination this researcher observes 100 examples and discovers that each one has a dark spot on its left ear. If he or she concludes that all such animals have a dark spot on the left ear, the validity of the conclusion depends on whether the researcher examined enough animals. Among thousands or millions of such animals in the world, it is doubtful that the researcher could reasonably conclude that they all share that characteristic (see Ziegelmueller and Dause on "numbers," 1975, p. 114).

Since it is usually difficult to examine every member of a population, it is more reasonable for a researcher to use a method of picking examples that will assure one of two alternatives: (1) A large portion or majority of the members of a population are examined, or (2) A method is used to compensate for the inability to examine a sufficient number. As mentioned in the discussion of statistical proof, the researcher may use a random sample or some type of representative sample.

REASONING FROM SIGN

This type of reasoning occurs when a speaker states or implies that the presence or existence of one thing or situation indicates the presence or existence of another thing or situation. A speaker indicates that local college students are not taking their studies seriously as evidenced by large crowds at the local bars. A "weather forecaster" warns people to prepare for a harsh winter, as caterpillars are fatter than normal, and squirrels have heavy coats of fur. This reasoning differs from causal reasoning in that one thing points to, indicates, or *suggests* something rather than actually *causes* it. Being in bars does not cause students to be uninterested in their studies but suggests that they are not. Caterpillars and squirrels do not cause severe winters but supposedly point to the coming of such winters.

When listening to this kind of reasoning, be aware of conditions that invalidate the assumption that one thing indicates the presence of something else. If, for example, someone says that increased troop movements and other military activities in a country indicate that the country is preparing to invade a neighboring country, you should consider that the activity might indicate something other than an approaching invasion. The country may be initiating new maneuvers for training purposes. Another possibility is that the country fears that the neighboring country is planning an attack. Or, this country could simply want the neighboring country to think they are preparing to invade.

There are, then, at least two tests for sign reasoning. First, a speaker might focus on only one sign while ignoring other relevant signs. Second, the speaker may concentrate on less important signs while ignoring signs that are more meaningful. A college admissions officer who considers only class rank in high school as a sign of success in college might ignore more important indicators such as size of the class, participation in extracurricular activities, test scores, unusual talents and abilities, and so forth (see Ziegelmueller and Dause, 1975, p. 119).

EVALUATING PROPAGANDA

Many, if not most, people probably respond negatively to propaganda as an evil, unethical type of emotional appeal deserving immediate and unqualified condemnation.

Before accepting such a negative view, however, consider a point of view expressed by Johannesen (1975), a scholar who has studied the ethics of communication extensively: Johannesen indicates that there are two views of propaganda. The first is neutral, defining propaganda as "an organized, continuous effort to persuade a mass audience primarily using the mass media" (pp. 73–74). Such methods may either be ethical or unethical, good or bad, depending on whether the persuasive efforts are grounded in solid evidence and reasoning. On the other hand, Johannesen indicates, propaganda does have a negative image. Viewed in this way it is defined as "the intentional use of suggestion, irrelevant emotional appeals, and pseudo-proof to circumvent human rational decision-making processes" (p. 74).

A repeated point in this book is the importance of making judgments and evaluations *after* making a sincere effort to understand. Thus, it seems more appropriate to suggest that you should approach propaganda as a neutral form of appeal, judging it to be wrong or unethical only after understanding it. If it represents an effort to circumvent reasoning and evidence, then it should probably be rejected. But if it appears to be used in conjunction with evidence and/or as a means of emphasizing and actualizing other forms of support, it might be accepted as a legitimate form of appeal (see Haiman, 1958, pp. 387–389). Johannesen provides an excellent example in his discussion of Harry Truman's whistle-stop campaign during the 1948 presidential election. The Institute for Propaganda Analysis considers the "plain folks" approach to be a propaganda technique: the speaker attempts to suggest to the audience that he or she is just a plain, ordinary person. While Truman used this technique, Johannesen presents two reasons why a listener might not condemn it. First, Truman used it as an introduction, not as a substitute for factual proof. Second, Mr. Truman was not necessarily deceptive. In many respects he actually *was* a person from common, ordinary origins and seemed never to have changed significantly in that respect. Thus, there is considerable difference between an ordinary person like Truman using plain folks appeals in contrast to a candidate who comes from a wealthy, privileged background (1975, pp. 74–75).

REFERENCES

Campbell, K. K. *Critiques of Contemporary Rhetoric.* Belmont, Calif.: Wadsworth, 1972.

Cathcart, R. *Post Communication: Rhetorical Analysis and Evaluation.* 2nd ed. Indianapolis: Bobbs-Merrill, 1981.

Ehninger, D. *Influence, Belief, and Argument: An Introduction to Responsible Persuasion.* Glenview, Ill.: Scott, Foresman, 1974.

Eisenberg, A. M. and J. A. Ilardo. *Argument: A Guide to Formal and Informal Debate.* 2nd ed. Englewood Cliffs, N.J.: Prentice-Hall, 1980.

Freeley, A. J. *Argumentation and Debate: Reasoned Decision Making.* 5th ed. Belmont, Calif.: Wadsworth, 1981.

Haiman, F. S. "Democratic Ethics and the Hidden Persuaders." *Quarterly Journal of Speech* 44 (1958), 385–392.

Johannesen, R. L. *Ethics in Human Communication*. Columbus, Ohio: Charles E. Merrill, 1975.

Larson, C. U. *Persuasion: Reception and Responsibility*. Belmont, Calif.: Wadsworth, 1973.

Ziegelmueller, G. W. and C. A. Dause. *Argumentation: Inquiry and Advocacy*. Englewood Cliffs, N.J.: Prentice-Hall, 1975.

KEY TERMS

Analysis

Evaluation

Suspension of judgment

Support

Factual support

Nonfactual support

Statistical support

Example

Real objects

Reasoning

Causal reasoning

Analogy

Reasoning from example

Reasoning from sign

Propaganda

EXERCISES

1. Listen to a recording or a video tape of a controversial speech. After hearing and/or seeing the speech, discuss it in small groups. Share your reactions and responses to the speech, particularly in relation to support material, reasoning, emotional appeal, and implied premises. At the end of the discussion period each group should report problems encountered, agreements and disagreements within the group, and any conclusions which the group members agreed to.

2. Each member of the class or group should locate examples of propaganda in mass media. Then share your findings and discuss what makes the material qualify as propaganda and whether it is ethical or unethical.

3. Write a paper in which you agree or disagree with Haiman's view of emotional appeal. If you agree, provide specific reasons and support for that stance. If you disagree, explain why and suggest an alternative point of view concerning emotional appeal.

4. Find a speech that interests you and examine it for specific uses of factual and nonfactual support, types of reasoning, and emotional appeals.

5. Divide into small groups and discuss your views concerning factors involved in evaluating messages. Try to reach as much agreement as possible concerning the *importance* of support, reasoning, emotional appeals, and ethics. Each group should report their findings and continue the discussion with the entire group or class.

CHAPTER

8

RESPONDING
THROUGH
FEEDBACK

OBJECTIVES

1. *To understand the difference between feedback in interpersonal settings and feedback in mass media settings.*
2. *To understand the nature of positive, negative, and neutral feedback.*
3. *To improve your ability to provide feedback clearly and effectively in a variety of listening situations.*

T he focus of this chapter is feedback as a listener response—and how it can contribute to effective communication. There are at least two reasons why feedback is an important listener function. First, feedback is an activity that listeners can contribute to almost any communication situation whether the speaker requests it or not. Second, it represents a means by which listeners can have a significant impact on the communication process. If you want to become a more effective listener you should understand and use feedback in a wide variety of listening situations.

SETTINGS FOR FEEDBACK

Although you may tend to think that feedback is restricted to face-to-face communication, it is possible to provide it in various mass media settings as well. Thus, you should consider feedback from two general perspectives—interpersonal and mass media. Let us examine the characteristics of each perspective.

INTERPERSONAL FEEDBACK

Miller (1966) defines interpersonal feedback as "those overt responses of a listener that serve to shape and to modify the succeeding communication behavior of the speaker" (p. 58). Such responses may be verbal or nonverbal and may exert both positive and negative influences on the speaker. As a result, the subsequent communication of the speaker and the listener may be affected. Feedback is thus "bidirectional and cumulative," meaning that the listener actually participates in and influences communication as it takes place (Schmidt and Graham, 1979, p. 3).

Consider the following situation: Two colleagues are discussing a project at work. One of them suggests a possible solution to a problem, and the other nods in agreement as the speaker is explaining his or her idea. This encourages the speaker to continue. Later in the discussion, however, the one who is listening responds by frowning and raising several questions that indicate confusion about or disagreement with something that was said. The speaker then attempts to clarify points that were unclear or unacceptable. This example briefly illustrates ways in which feedback enables people to facilitate communication by monitoring each other's behavior.

FEEDBACK AND MASS MEDIA

Essentially, feedback presented to speakers who communicate on television, radio, and movies is indirect. Obviously, you cannot directly influence a person talking on television from hundreds or even thousands of miles away. You can, however, provide indirect feedback in the form of letters, telephone calls, purchasing or refusing to purchase products, voting, continuing or refusing to watch programs, and talking or writing to those who are in a position to relay your responses to those who produce and/or sponsor various messages and programs. On the other hand, producers, sponsors, and participants frequently seek feedback from listeners through surveys, call-in programs, and promotional devices such as sweepstakes and other types of prizes and incentives.

As an illustration of the impact that listeners/viewers can have, consider that several years ago the popular television show "Star Trek" was about to be taken off the air. An overwhelming negative response from viewers caused the producers and the network to continue airing the show. When there is widespread negative response to commercials and sales drop, you can be certain that the commercials will change. And during the 1976 presidential campaign, President Gerald R. Ford carelessly stated, during a televised debate with Jimmy Carter, that countries in Eastern Europe are not controlled by the Soviet Union; not surprisingly, the negative response from viewers was unmistakable.

In the future, feedback to mass media will become increasingly widespread and direct. With the ongoing development of computers, more avenues will open for inviting, receiving, storing, and using audience feedback. In some areas of the United States experimental systems permit television viewers to provide immediate and direct feedback to television programs. There is reason to believe that such techniques will be developed to the point that you can expect more, rather than less, opportunity to supply feedback to the mass media.

TYPES OF FEEDBACK

There are three types of feedback: *positive, negative,* and *neutral.* Each type can be presented verbally or nonverbally as listeners attempt to influence speakers and their messages.

POSITIVE FEEDBACK

Positive feedback expresses agreement, approval, understanding, or acceptance of the speaker and/or message. Applause, cheers, standing ovations, smiles, head nods, and encouraging comments are examples of positive feedback. Such feedback provides positive reinforcement for the speaker. Skinner (1953) indicates that positive reinforcement increases the probability that a person will continue the behavior. Thus, positive feedback encourages the speaker. It is difficult to imagine speakers who do not appreciate positive feedback.

NEGATIVE FEEDBACK

Negative feedback consists of verbal and nonverbal messages of disapproval, disagreement, and rejection of speakers and/or messages. Verbal statements like "That's stupid" or "You don't know what you're talking about" are examples of negative feedback. Nonverbally, a sarcastic tone of voice, clenched fists, down-turned thumbs, frowns, boos, throwing of objects, interrupting, leaving the room, signs, and so on constitute negative feedback.

It is unreasonable to assert that negative feedback is always undesirable and never useful. You should, however, consider the implications of using it. Ask yourself these questions about negative feedback: Does it encourage or discourage effective communication between people? Does it encourage people to respond defensively? Is it more constructive or destructive? Do you like to receive negative responses from other people?

NEUTRAL FEEDBACK

Neutral feedback is essentially nonevaluative. You can use it to seek clarification or to indicate confusion, not as a means of "punishing" the speaker but as a means of helping him or her to communicate as effectively as possible. You might ask a speaker to define a word or to repeat an explanation. You can shrug your shoulders to indicate that you don't understand. Neutral feedback can also enable you to indicate that a message *is* clear and understandable. It can also be used to check your interpretation of what a speaker has said. You might say, for example, "Here is what I think you mean." This gives a speaker an opportunity to know that you understand or to clear up a misunderstanding.

There is no doubt that the differences between neutral and positive or negative feedback are not always clear. Since people attach meanings to symbols, the speaker might interpret the feedback as positive or negative when you intended it to be neutral. Such problems can never be avoided totally, but your efforts to send feedback as clearly and honestly as possible will help to minimize misunderstandings.

PROVIDING FEEDBACK EFFECTIVELY

The participatory nature of feedback suggests that it is to your advantage to convey it as effectively as possible. As Howell and Bormann (1971) point out, nonparticipatory, noninteractive speaking is almost always characterized by "a total absence of feedback" (p. 283). As a listener, therefore, your ability to respond with useful feedback can contribute significantly to better communication. The eight suggestions which follow are guidelines for improving the quality of your feedback.

1. BE INTENTIONAL AND HONEST

To the extent that your feedback confuses or misleads the speaker, its value is diminished or destroyed. Laughing to indicate lack of understanding, for example, could cause a speaker to feel that you are laughing at him or her. It might also suggest that you are rejecting the message. Looking down and away from the speaker could indicate anger, lack of interest, disgust, or embarrassment, for example. As a listener you should make every effort to avoid sending ambiguous feedback.

It is also possible for a listener to provide various forms of dishonest feedback. Faking attention, pretending to be interested, feigning agreement are examples of behavior that produces dishonest feedback. Whether done to be polite, to conform to the behavior of others, to avoid being called on, or for other reasons, such feedback seldom contributes to attention, to understanding, or to fair evaluation.

Even worse is the use of feedback as a means of distracting the speaker, making a mockery of the situation, or drawing attention to oneself. This type of feedback might consist of pointless questions, attempts to get the speaker off the subject, or arguing for the sake of argument. It has no place in effective listening.

It is sometimes said that people cannot *not* communicate. It may also be true, in a sense, that listeners cannot *not* provide feedback. But it is not sufficient to give feedback by default, inaction, or uncertainty. Effective listeners should attempt to present feedback directly, intentionally, and honestly.

2. PROVIDE NEGATIVE FEEDBACK SPARINGLY

The suggestion to provide negative feedback sparingly does not mean that you should never use it. Sometimes you encounter speakers who attempt to trick, confuse, or deceive listeners, and you may decide that such speakers deserve negative feedback. You might conclude, also, that negative feedback is an honest way to tell a speaker that he or she is doing a poor job of communicating, is uninformed, mistaken, and so forth.

When you feel that negative feedback is appropriate, you should make certain that you have attended to, understood, and carefully evaluated the message *prior* to responding negatively. If not, you run the risk of falling victim to undesirable listening practices like the entertainment syndrome, listening with your biases, or the desire to talk rather than to listen. Negative feedback certainly should not be conveyed unless you have thoroughly and fairly evaluated the message.

Although negative feedback can encourage a speaker to adjust to listener needs, to restate a position, clarify meaning, and so on, it frequently leads to anger, defensiveness, and retaliation. By providing neutral feedback you may accomplish your purpose without evoking such responses from a speaker. A listener who asks, "When you say that Sue dislikes you what, specifically, has she said that makes you feel that way?" elicits information and explanation from the speaker. But the listener who says, "Stop feeling sorry for yourself. Sometimes you seem downright paranoid," is probably going to succeed only in angering the speaker. You are encouraged, therefore, to examine your reasons, motives, and the desired outcome before providing negative feedback.

Listening Lab

Improving Your Ability to Use Feedback Effectively

* Provide feedback intentionally and honestly
* Be independent when providing feedback
* Use both verbal and nonverbal feedback
* Use negative feedback sparingly and purposefully
* Direct feedback to messages rather than to speakers
* When speakers respond (or fail to respond) to feedback, provide follow-up feedback
* Don't assume that speakers will respond in a particular way to your feedback

3. DIRECT FEEDBACK TO MESSAGES NOT SPEAKERS

It is perhaps a natural tendency to react to people rather than to their ideas. But in providing feedback it is preferable to respond to ideas rather than to people. When feedback is directed toward speakers it often suggests the functioning of various preconceptions. For example, one could declare that anyone from a certain political party, occupation, ethnic group, and so on cannot be worth listening to *or* that anything he or she says is automatically true or valuable. In a recent campus speech, the speaker was well known and rather infamous. Advertisements for this speaker tended to focus on his name and past experiences rather than on his topic. The speaker was G. Gordon Liddy, convicted Watergate burglar and Nixon associate. Prior to Liddy's appearance a group of people distributed pamphlets and leaflets urging others not to attend the speech and vigorously protesting the use of university funds to bring this speaker to campus. Inside the auditorium was a group of people dressed in outlandish outfits, such as clothing made from an American flag. These people had numerous signs with derogatory messages about the speaker. As soon as Liddy appeared they held up their signs and repeatedly interrupted the speaker.

There are probably a number of arguments that can be made in defense of such responses to Liddy or to other speakers whom people decide are dangerous, evil, mistaken, misguided, and so on. Nonetheless, this kind of feedback expresses evaluations made *prior* to attending and understanding the speaker's message. It also appears to involve a refusal to set biases aside. It is unlikely that the protestors paid close attention to Liddy's speech or made much of an effort to understand it. And the people urging others not to attend the speech were advocating the condemnation of a speech before a word had been spoken. It is difficult to conclude that these behaviors represent effective listening. There is no law that says that everything spoken by "good," acceptable speakers is true and just; nor is there a law that says that everything a "bad" or disagreeable person says is wrong. And it does not follow necessarily that a speaker is going to present the same message each time he or she speaks. The obligation of effective listeners should be to provide feedback in response to their efforts to understand and evaluate the message rather than the speaker.

4. PROVIDE FOLLOW-UP FEEDBACK

Effective listeners are patient and persistent. It is usually desirable, therefore, for you to follow one feedback message with another and, at times, another and another. Some speakers may be annoyed with such a practice, but when your feedback is honestly and clearly presented it should function to improve communication between you and the speaker. Since feedback is one of the best means of enhancing understanding, if a speaker's answer to a question is not clear, ask another question. If one statement appears to contradict another, express your confusion verbally and/or nonverbally. As long as such feedback is presented in a fair and courteous manner, it represents a useful attempt to listen effectively. You are encouraged to use follow-up feedback and to do so even if some people view it as a nuisance or waste of time.

5. DO NOT ANTICIPATE SPEAKER RESPONSES

Your attempts to provide feedback as a means of participating constructively in the communication process can be damaged or defeated if you fall into the practice of anticipating the speaker's responses. If you think, for example, that a question or statement will force the speaker to respond in a certain way or to make a specific statement, it is possible that you will selectively perceive the response, *making* it, in effect, whatever you expected it to be.

The way in which you listen to a speaker's responses to your feedback is just as important as any other aspect of listening. Imagine a situation in which you listen carefully to another person, spot an area of confusion or contradiction, provide feedback, and then fail to listen carefully and accurately to the response. Or, assume that you are convinced that a friend's response to your attempt to point out a contradiction will be angry and resentful. If you are not careful, you may "read" anger and resentment into the other person's response. As a listener, then, you must face the challenging task of recognizing your own listening problems throughout a communication event. The point is clear: listening to another's response to your feedback requires the same effort as listening to any other portion of a message.

6. REINFORCE SPEAKERS WHO RESPOND TO YOUR FEEDBACK

While it can be frustrating and discouraging when someone seems unwilling to respond to your feedback, it is highly rewarding when your feedback is acknowledged and responded to. Thus you should attempt to give positive feedback in acknowledgment of a speaker's willingness to respond. Since communication is an interactive process, it follows that listeners can encourage speakers just as speakers can adapt to and encourage listeners. If you smile and thank someone for his or her responses, what person is going to feel discouraged and unwilling to exert an even greater effort to communicate effectively?

7. USE FEEDBACK INDEPENDENTLY

Feedback should occur because listeners feel the need to respond to speakers' messages. Your feedback should not be determined by other listeners. If you feel that a speaker's message is not deserving of a standing ovation, there is no reason why you must provide such feedback—even when other listeners do so. If some people interrupt a speaker, or respond with other forms of negative feedback, you are certainly not obligated to do so. Similarly, you should not hesitate to ask a question merely because no one else is willing to ask one.

This does not mean that you will be unaffected by those around you, or that you will not get caught up in the responses of other people. If you feel the same way, join the group's efforts. It does not mean, either, that you should make a point of being different, or that it is necessarily undesirable to participate in a response like polite applause for someone who has made an honest effort to communicate. Essentially, however, feedback should represent your individual responses to the message. Mindlessly going along with the crowd makes no more sense in listening than in any other activity.

8. COMBINE VERBAL AND NONVERBAL FEEDBACK

You can increase the likelihood that your feedback will be clearer and more effective by coordinating verbal and nonverbal aspects of your feedback. As Shakespeare expressed it, "suit the action to the word." It is confusing to a speaker when your verbal feedback appears to communicate one thing, and your nonverbal feedback says something else. Gestures, facial expressions, posture, eye contact, and so on can help you emphasize and clarify your verbal feedback. While there are situations in which verbal feedback is inappropriate or difficult to use, the ideal situation is probably one in which you can use both types. As a listener who is attempting to contribute to effective communication, do not hesitate to combine verbal and nonverbal feedback whenever possible.

REFERENCES

Howell, W. S. and E. G. Bormann. *Presentational Speaking for Business and the Professions.* New York: Harper and Row, 1971.

Miller, G. *Speech Communication: A Behavioral Approach.* Indianapolis: Bobbs-Merrill, 1966.

Schmidt, W. and J. Graham. *The Public Forum: A Transactional Approach.* Sherman Oaks, Calif.: Alfred Publishing, 1979.

Skinner, B. F. *Science and Human Behavior.* New York: Macmillan, 1953.

KEY TERMS

Feedback

Interpersonal feedback

Mass media feedback

Positive feedback

Negative feedback

Neutral feedback

Nonverbal feedback

Verbal feedback

EXERCISES

1. Attend a lecture or public speech of your choice or as assigned by your instructor. Observe the audience members' use of feedback as well as the speaker's responses to it. Describe, analyze, and evaluate the use of feedback in the situation which you observed.

2. Meet in small groups and assign the following roles: (a) Negative Feedback Giver, (b) Argumentative Feedback Giver, (c) Positive Feedback Giver, and (d) Neutral Feedback Giver. Each person should initiate a conversation on a controversial subject with a friend. He or she should play the assigned feedback role in the conversation. Report the results observed for comparison and discussion.

3. Using a geometric design, one person can volunteer to instruct the rest of the group on how to reproduce the geometric design. In the first attempt, class

members should turn their backs toward the volunteer, allowing him or her to give oral instructions (no audience feedback allowed). In the second attempt the class members should face the speaker and be allowed to use verbal and nonverbal feedback during the giving of instructions. Compare the results of efforts 1 and 2. Discuss differences between the two attempts.

4. Listen to an informative message. Half of the group will listen to the tape in one room, while the other half of the group listens to the speech delivered in person. Compare scores on a test over the information presented in the speech and analyze the differences.

5. In a discussion with a friend or a group of friends, attempt to provide no feedback whatever. Note any reactions or responses.

C H A P T E R

9

RESPONDING
EMPATHICALLY

OBJECTIVES

1. *To understand the nature of empathic listening.*
2. *To understand the difference between monologic and dialogic communication.*
3. *To apply dialogic concepts to your listening as a means of moving toward empathic listening in a variety of communication settings.*
4. *To appreciate and strive to achieve the advantages of empathic listening.*

Empathic listening is an extremely important kind of listening. Often identified with interpersonal and therapeutic listening, it requires that you strive to respond to others from an attitude of genuine concern and involvement. Empathic listening relates to daily communication situations—between husbands and wives, parents and children, friends, neighbors, and colleagues. By improving your ability to respond empathically you can enhance your ability to establish, strengthen, and sustain relationships. And since empathic listening represents an attitude toward speakers, you can extend it to almost any type of listening.

EMPATHIC LISTENING DEFINED

Stewart (1977) emphasizes that empathic listening "is one of those elements of interpersonal communication that looks easy on paper but is seldom practiced effectively" (p. 222). He points out that attempts to listen empathically usually disappear whenever the conversation or speech becomes "interesting" or "threatening." If neither of these conditions occurs, people may simply respond to speakers mechanically and insincerely, only pretending to listen emphatically (p. 222). This suggests that empathic listening is more than a set of rules, procedures, or mechanical behaviors. It is, instead, an *attitudinal, motivational approach to listening.*

Empathy is a matter of feeling *with* the other person. It is more than simply understanding or evaluating another person's message, for the empathic listener should actively strive to "appreciate" the other's feelings "as he or she feels them" (Brown and Keller, 1979, pp. 12–13). Thus, listening empathically requires that you demonstrate an understanding and appreciation of the speaker's meanings from an emotional perspective as well as a literal one.

A major difficulty with empathic listening is presented by Martin Buber (1970). He contends that you do not *experience* another person; when you attempt to experience, analyze, or understand another, the true relationship is lost or nonexistent (pp. 59–61, pp. 74–75). Specifically, Buber indicates that a genuine empathy (or coming together of two persons) defies understanding: Whenever one attempts to analyze and describe an empathic relationship objectively, that relationship is essentially lost. It simply cannot be studied in a scientific sense (p. 91).

If Buber is correct, and empathic listening is a mysterious process of human relationships, you may justifiably ask how it can be described without violating its very nature. Johannesen (1971) raises this question when he asks whether one can actually observe, describe, or study such communication without violating its nature and functions. While there is no easy or simple answer to this question, it does serve as a reminder that empathic listening is difficult to understand and practice. You must do more than give the appearance of interest, concern, and involvement, and you must avoid allowing phrases, jargon, and technical terminology to substitute for empathic listening.

Since the nature of empathy precludes a rule-oriented approach to responding empathically, it is necessary that you acquire *attitudes* toward communication that will enable you to move toward empathic listening. A discussion of monologue and dialogue will serve as a starting point.

DIALOGUE VERSUS MONOLOGUE

You may think of monologue as characterizing situations in which one person does all or most of the talking while others listen passively. On the other hand, you may view dialogue as an exchange in which speakers and listeners switch roles in a give-and-take fashion. You might also view these as theatrical terms to describe the difference between a situation in which an actor or actress presents long, uninterrupted speeches in contrast to those situations in which the characters in a play exchange lines as in conversation.

As used here, however, monologue and dialogue are used in a different sense than either of the above definitions. Specifically, monologue represents communication that "seeks to command, coerce, manipulate, conquer, dazzle, deceive, or exploit" (Johannesen, 1971, p. 377). Dialogue, in contrast, is an attitude toward, or approach to, communication "characterized by such qualities as mutuality, open-heartedness, directness, honesty, spontaneity, frankness, lack of pretense, nonmanipulative intent, communion, intensity, and love in the sense of responsibility of one human for another" (Johannesen, 1971, p. 375).

Perhaps the key to dialogic communication is that the speaker strives to recognize and to minimize his or her tendencies toward selfishness and manipulation. Monologue, on the other hand, is communication that either ignores such tendencies or is intentionally designed for selfish, manipulative purposes. Either approach can be adopted by a speaker—regardless of the communication setting.

To this point, the discussion of monologue and dialogue has focused primarily on the speaker. You can, however, just as readily apply these concepts to the role of the listener. At the very least, empathy is a critical attribute of dialogic listening. It is difficult to imagine that you could listen dialogically and not respond to the speaker empathically. And while speakers must satisfy certain criteria in order to qualify as dialogic, it is equally necessary that listeners do their part to achieve dialogic communication.

MONOLOGIC LISTENING

A monologic listener can be expected to exhibit the same attitudes and behaviors toward speakers that monologic speakers exhibit toward listeners. Rather than putting himself or herself in the place of the speaker, a monologic listener tends to view the speaker as someone to be used; to be taken advantage of for self-serving purposes. Such a listener might view the speaker as an adversary, or as someone to be used, manipulated, taken advantage of, or ignored. The monologic listener tends to disagree and argue prior to understanding the speaker. Confidential information, admissions of weakness, or personal problems can serve to provide a monologic listener with "ammunition" to be used against the speaker. In short, the monologic listener has little concern for the speaker, makes little effort to respond to a speech or conversation from the speaker's perspective, and views the listening situation as an opportunity to take advantage of the speaker. Such a listener responds to speakers selfishly and unfairly.

DIALOGIC LISTENING

As previously discussed, empathic listening and dialogue are closely related if not one and the same concept. When Johannesen (1971) presents the characteristics of dialogue, for example, he in no way suggests that they apply exclusively to the speaker. On the contrary, he discusses these characteristics in language that implies two or more people engaged in interaction. Those characteristics are:

> (1) Genuineness, (2) Accurate Empathic Understanding, (3) Unconditional Positive Regard, (4) Presentness, (5) Spirit of Mutual Equality, and (6) Supportive Psychological Climate. (p. 376)

GENUINENESS

Genuineness means that you listen without deception. You are not genuine when you provide feedback that is insincere or when you pretend interest in a speaker's ideas and feelings while really not caring. To pretend interest in a speaker's problems, activities, disappointments, and so on hardly qualifies as responding empathically. In contrast, a genuine listener responds honestly, avoids jumping to conclusions, judging the speaker, or "using" him or her for selfish reasons. Ideally, the speaker should be able to talk to you as you are, not to an artificial, disguised version of yourself.

ACCURATE EMPATHIC UNDERSTANDING

Empathic understanding means that you should make every effort to place yourself in the speaker's position. Avoid being a detached, disinterested observer. Understand the speaker rather than judging or evaluating him or her. To achieve empathic understanding you should provide feedback that enables the speaker to agree to or correct your interpretations of the message. It is exciting to imagine how drastically improved communication could be if listeners actively pursued such understanding of speakers.

UNCONDITIONAL POSITIVE REGARD

You may feel that this quality of empathic listening is difficult to grasp or to accept. It means that you should accept the speaker as a person of unquestioned worth simply because he or she is a human being. Some people have trouble accepting this notion—even as an ideal or goal. But this criterion does not mean that all people are equally good, kind, productive, honest, likeable, or acceptable. It does mean that you respond to speakers as having value simply because they are human.

Thinking of others as objects or roles has a dehumanizing effect. During the "protest years" of the late 1960s and early 1970s, it was not uncommon for antagonistic individuals and groups to respond to others in this way. Police were "pigs." Conservatives were "fascist pigs." Older people sometimes referred to young people as "longhaired freaks." It is easier to throw things at people, avoid contact with them, club them over the head, or even kill them if they

---

Listening Lab

Improving Your Ability to Listen Empathically

* Strive to develop a positive, caring attitude

* Apply dialogic principles to your listening in a variety of situations

* Reduce or eliminate monologic tendencies in your listening

* Avoid the tendency to talk rather than listen

* Resist the temptation to judge or give advice

* Provide feedback which will encourage further communication

are first dehumanized. Some people believe that such tactics are necessary and serve useful purposes, but it is difficult to imagine that they produce meaningful dialogue.

PRESENTNESS

Presentness applies to much of the discussion of listening throughout this book. Essentially, it means that you actively attend to the speaker, that you stay with him or her as you listen. You can be in the room, sitting next to or across from the speaker but not really present. Your thoughts and attention can be elsewhere. Daydreaming is a good example of the lack of presentness in listening.

The absence of presentness adversely affects attention, diminishes your ability to understand, and hampers your ability to evaluate fairly. To achieve presentness in your listening you need to apply repeatedly the three steps of recognition, refusal, and replacement. Without presentness you cannot respond effectively to any speaker.

SPIRIT OF MUTUAL EQUALITY

A spirit of mutual equality must not be misunderstood to mean that everyone is equal. Instead, it suggests that you attempt to listen to others from an orientation of equality in the sense that everyone has the right to communicate freely and openly. If you allow your biases to determine that some people's ideas are inherently inferior (or superior) you will probably destroy the chance for empathic listening. A person of superior knowledge or accomplishments demeans himself or herself by assuming that another person can say little or nothing of value or importance. Similarly, you can hardly expect to respond empathically if you feel inferior to the other person.

Experience demonstrates that people are capable of wisdom and folly—regardless of who they are or what they have accomplished. A spirit of equality in communication implies, then, that you encourage the other person to speak without prior evaluation or other restrictions. After understanding someone, you certainly have the right to evaluate, to accept, or to reject his or her ideas. It is far less clear that you should evaluate another's feelings.

SUPPORTIVE PSYCHOLOGICAL CLIMATE

This criterion contributes to a cumulative effect of your efforts to respond empathically. It suggests that you convey to the speaker that you are *for* him or her rather than *against* him or her. In short, to the extent that you respond genuinely, accurately, positively, with presentness, and in a spirit of mutual equality, you will move toward the establishment of a supportive psychological climate. In such a climate people feel free to express themselves openly and honestly without fear of being attacked or berated. They can expect listeners to make an honest effort to hear them out. In such a climate speakers feel encouraged to speak.

AN ILLUSTRATION OF EMPATHIC LISTENING

Empathic listening is particularly valuable in a special type of listening that is sometimes referred to as "therapeutic" listening (Wolvin and Coakley, 1979). The purpose of such listening is to help other people to express their true feelings and, consequently, to solve their own problems. It is listening that places definite demands on the listener, as he or she must strive to assume a helping attitude, acting as a "sounding board" for others (Wolvin and Coakley, 1982, p. 109). To accomplish this attitude, you must avoid the temptation to dominate or control the speaker. When practiced effectively, this approach to listening will enable you to respond empathically and to make valuable contributions to others in a variety of interpersonal settings.

A DEFINITION OF ACTIVE LISTENING

Carl Rogers and Richard Farson (1969) stress that "active listening" is a means to fulfilling the listening function described above. Rather than listening passively, the active listener makes a concentrated effort to grasp as fully as possible the "facts and feelings in what he hears" as a means of helping the speaker to "work out his own problems." Such listening requires an attitude of respect for the speaker as a person of "potential worth." Additionally, it requires a belief in the speaker as one who is capable of "self-direction" (pp. 480–482).

As you consider what Rogers and Farson have said about active listening, you will see how dialogic principles apply to situations in which you can serve as a therapeutic listener. Attitudes such as an unconditional positive regard, accurate empathic understanding, and a spirit of mutual equality are particularly applicable to this kind of listening.

HOW TO LISTEN ACTIVELY

Rogers and Farson stress that active listening demands a willingness to allow the speaker to understand his or her self-image: rather than attempting to force the speaker to become defensive about his or her thoughts and feelings, you make no effort to threaten the other's self-concept, allowing him or her to "explore it, see it for what it is, make his own decision about how realistic it is" and then work toward changing it (Rogers and Farson, pp. 482–484).

Let's consider a situation in which two co-workers are talking about their boss. One of them says, "It isn't right. Jones likes to push me around. Just because she's a department manager, she doesn't have the right to talk down to me all the time." The other person replies, "Oh come on. Jones isn't any different in the way she treats you. She's just as demanding with me." In this situation, the listener has not attempted to listen empathically but has responded by chastising the other person. The speaker's feelings are immediately interpreted from the listener's perspective.

On the other hand, this listener might have responded by saying, "It sounds like Jones is really getting to you. You probably feel like you can't do anything to please her." This response gives the speaker an opportunity to explore his or her feelings further and to decide whether the listener's statements actually reflect how he or she feels. The listener has invited additional communication, additional expressions of feeling, without forcing the speaker into a defensive posture. Consequently, the listener has increased the chances that the speaker can solve his or her problems.

ADVANTAGES TO THE LISTENER

Empathic listening definitely benefits the listener, providing him or her with an opportunity to grow beyond the limitations of his or her personal views by "seeing" things from the other's perspective. In turn, the listener can make constructive changes in his or her self-image. As Rogers and Farson state, you must be willing to take a risk. By opening yourself to the feelings and views of another person you risk being changed, and this can be extremely threatening (Rogers and Farson, pp. 489–490).

I hope that you are willing to take such a risk. If you do, you will discover that your listening will help others and yourself. On the interpersonal level, you may discover that these are the most rewarding of all the benefits which accrue from improving your listening abilities.

REFERENCES

Brown, C. T. and P. W. Keller. *Monologue to Dialogue: An Exploration of Interpersonal Communication.* 2nd ed. Englewood Cliffs, N.J.: Prentice-Hall, 1979.

Buber, M. *I and Thou.* W. Kaufmann, trans. New York: Charles Scribner's Sons, 1970.

Johannesen, R. L. "The Emerging Concept of Communication as Dialogue." *Quarterly Journal of Speech* 57 (1971), 373–382.

Rogers, C. R. and R. E. Farson. "Active Listening." In *Readings in Interpersonal and Organizational Communication,* R. C. Huseman et al., eds. Boston: Holbrook Press, 1969, 480–496.

Stewart, J. *Bridges Not Walls.* 2nd ed. Reading, Mass.: Addison-Wesley, 1977.

Wolvin, A. D. and C. G. Coakley. *Listening Instruction.* Urbana, Ill.: ERIC Clearinghouse on Reading and Communication Skills, 1979.

Wolvin, A. D. and C. G. Coakley. *Listening.* Dubuque, Iowa: Wm. C. Brown, 1982.

KEY TERMS

Empathy

Dialogue

Monologue

Genuineness

Unconditional positive regard

Presentness

Spirit of mutual equality

Supportive psychological climate

Active listening

EXERCISES

1. Divide into groups of two. Each partner should write down assumptions that he or she has about the other person. Share these assumptions and discuss their accuracy.

2. After listening to a lecture or speech presented by someone you find unlikable, mistaken, boring, incompetent, etc., prepare a list of what you disliked about the speaker. In a group discussion share your responses. Also discuss ways in which you allowed negative attitudes toward the speaker to interfere with your understanding of the speaker's message.

3. Select a current, controversial issue. Read the letters to the editor section of a newspaper and clip letters that express anger and hostility toward individuals such as public officials. Search, also, for letters that are critical but avoid making personal attacks. Ask

someone to read passages from these letters. In a discussion point out major differences in the two types of letters. Discuss ways in which personal attacks prevent understanding and appreciation of another person's position.

4. For approximately one week make a conscious effort to listen to your friends with the intention of understanding and appreciating their feelings, attitudes, problems, accomplishments, and so forth. Try to provide feedback which is positive, seeks clarification, and encourages them to express themselves.

5. In group discussions exchange ideas about a controversial topic. Allow everyone complete freedom to speak—with one exception. Before contributing to the discussion each speaker must paraphrase the statement of the previous speaker.

I N D E X